With 367 illustrations, 290 in colour

**On the cover:** Foster and Partners' Great Glass House, National
Botanic Garden of Wales, UK (photo Nigel Young/Foster and Partners).
**Back, clockwise from top left** Dominique Perrault's Olympic Velodrome,
Berlin, Germany (photo © ADAGP, Paris and DACS, London 2002; Christian
Richters); Peter Zumthor's Thermal Baths, Vals, Switzerland (photo
Christian Richters); Ian Ritchie Architects' Crystal Palace Concert
Platform, London, UK (photo Jocelyne Van den Bossche); Morphosis's
Diamond Ranch High School, Pomona, US (photo Timothy Hursley)

**p. 1** Antoine Predock's Spencer Theater, Ruidoso, US (photo Timothy Hursley)
**p. 3** Future Systems' House in Wales, UK (photo Richard Davies)

First published in the United Kingdom in 2002 by
Thames & Hudson Ltd, 181A High Holborn, London WC1V 7QX

www.thamesandhudson.com

© 2002 Aaron Betsky
This edition 2005

British Library Cataloguing-in-Publication Data
A catalogue record for this book is available from the
British Library
ISBN-13:  978-0-500-34217-6
ISBN-10:  0-500-34217-2

Designed by SMITH, London

Printed and bound in Singapore by Star Standard
Industries Pte Ltd

# landscrapers

## building with the land aaron betsky

Thames & Hudson

Buildings replace the land. That is architecture's original sin. A building makes something new, but does not do so in a void. What was once open land, filled with sunlight and air, with a distinct relationship to the horizon, becomes a building. The artifices of humans supersede what nature has deposited on a given place. The bulk of a building stops air, sunlight and views. The memories that we built up around that particular place, either individually or as a culture, also disappear. In their place is a structure that is new, if only for a moment, and that aspires to have a perfect form, function and appearance. Some buildings even hope to move as far away as possible from the land on which they rise. In all cases, a building is one thing above all else: not the land.

To some, architecture is the thoughtful gathering together of what already exists to reveal the nature of a place. Others merely replace the land with something that is as new and artificial as any building, but which continues the contours or appearance of the land. There are even those who see their task not so much as building on the land as building into it. Makers of caves and caverns, these designers continue a long tradition of inhabiting or enlarging the spaces left over by the accumulation of sediment and the shift of tectonic plates. At the other extreme are buildings that hover over the ground, following its contours and abstracting them into sometimes massive buildings. All these strategies represent an attitude that is contrary to what has been one of the most basic and least popular mainstays of architecture since the days of the Romans: to deny the land on which we build. This book, however, presents buildings that seek to restore the land and architects that see their work as unfolding the land rather than hiding it.

The sins of architecture emerge from its very nature as an artificial construction, but are also the result of why and how we have built over the centuries. The act of making a building assumes that the land we walk on is not enough. We must enclose a space with walls, smooth the surface, and put a roof over our heads to protect ourselves from the elements.[1] These are all essentially defensive acts: the land ceases to be just a place and becomes a territory, something that we can define as our property and thus must defend against others. Making a building is like putting on clothes in that we suppose our own skin is not the proper or adequate way to appear; instead we must form a second skin, present a mask to the outside world, and enlarge what we are by creating space. In that sense, it is also a mark of our sin.

When we started to build as a society and not just as individuals, this sense of defense was taken much further.

Vitruvius, the first codifier of the rules of architecture, began his famous treatise *De Architectura*[2] (ten books on architecture) by referring to architecture as an aspect of defense. The enemy was not just an outside group that might want to attack, it was also the diseases that might come from the ground and the chilly vapors that might rise out of it. It was the heat that might come from the sky and, though this was never said by Vitruvius or any other early theoretician, the sheer expanse of space from which the nascent urban environment distinguished itself.[3]

When architecture was not defensive, it was defiant. Standing against the mountains, the seas, unformed expanses of land and the scale of the sky, temples and cultural institutions sought to bring a sense of order to the unbounded universe. Greek temples stood tall against the land and were the mark of a human civilization that saw the land as potential colonies. The temples represented hidden divinities and forces that were not evident in the land itself, but that human beings invented as ways of making sense of places, naming them and constructing narratives about them. The Greek temples and cities that spread throughout the Mediterranean area spoke of otherness, difference and the artifice of human culture.[4]

Through the ages, we have continued to make buildings with this in mind. Our castles, palaces, churches and libraries are celebrations of all that is not nature. They are monuments to our ability to gather material, often from far away, form it according to abstract principles and make buildings that stand tall and proud while sheltering an interior that is rational and functional. Our cities, which create their own labyrinthine order on the land, often grow higher century by century as we deposit the detritus of our lives in ever-thicker layers and rise further and further above the ground. Skyscrapers signal our competitive desire to build higher for no other reason than to offer more space and a better image. Defense has been sublimated into strange and tall forms.

Yet nature always creeps in. In the basements, where the foundations of our most skyward-reaching ambitions rest on the land we attempt to deny, the reality becomes evident. We are afraid of these dark places. Their smell and damp seep into the gridded rooms above. They remind us of what we have buried, and so we associate them with the act of internment. In fiction, they are the places where what we thought we had left behind or conquered rises up again to take its often terrible revenge on us. The higher we build, the more we sense our dislocation. A fear of heights increases as we spiral ever further away from the land.[5]

In recent years, we have once again become more aware of the reality of the land. Guilt now pervades much of our culture. Perhaps it comes from a sense of what we have lost, a romantic desire to recapture the land. This ideal has been a staple of our cultural efforts since at least the eighteenth century and the Rousseauian move back to nature, though it has its roots in much older tracts, such as Lucius Annaeus Seneca's *Epistles*.[6] We ascribe mythical qualities to the land, and refer to it in even our most frivolous decorations—bringing stylized versions of plants and animals into our homes in wallpaper, paintings or little figurines.[7] In architecture, the notion that a building should open itself back up to nature has led some designers and theoreticians to call for what they term an "organic" architecture, a way of making a building that eschews man-made materials and unfolds according to the logic of our lives. It would be in one piece, as if the building were an organism that grew, rather than being constructed on a place.[8]

Much of the impetus for this kind of building comes from the realization that our uses of the land have not all been beneficial. We have raped the land as much as we have used it. As we have depleted open space and natural resources, we have left the land scarred, empty and often poisonous. Even when we build wisely on a given spot, respecting the land as much as possible, the materials we use denude forests, gouge quarries in mountains or convert the wealth of the land into artificial materials through the use of refineries or smelting plants that are themselves usually ruinous eyesores.

In many European countries, these conditions have encouraged governments to try to make buildings more responsive to the landscape. This has led not only to the re-emergence of operable windows and the introduction of less harmful materials, but also to the insertion of gardens in skyscrapers, or the use of grass as an insulating roof.[9] Architects have been forced to rethink their buildings' forms. If the roof is made out of grass, why not make it habitable? To do so, there should be a relationship, preferably direct and physical, with the land around the structure. The result is such devices as the sloping roof of the Central Library in Delft (1992–97, see p. 108), designed by Dutch firm Mecanoo.

Building with the land is not just the result of ecological concerns, nor are all architects suddenly gripped by a back-to-the-land fervor. There is also a sense that we have misconceived the nature of building. Drawing on an ancient tradition of hidden or secret architecture, theoreticians have long been proposing alternatives to the defensive structures and attitudes we associate with architecture. They point out that to this day some people still live in caves, and we are continually fascinated by their possibilities. They represent the beginnings of art (cave paintings) and they provide the refuge from which spirituality is born. It is as if, by going into the earth, we find the wisdom we then use to impose ourselves upon it. Whether one uncovers Delphic riddles or luminous marks of the hunt in the cave, the hidden treasures give meaning to the rational work outside.

It might even be true that we aim to make many of our spaces into caves to create a sense of comfort or belonging. The designed interior, which forms an artificial world within the walls of architecture, often evokes the land through its imagery and forms.

It is no coincidence that the styles we most associate with interior decoration, such as Rococo and Arts and Crafts, are the ones that most frequently bring flowers, trees and other elements of nature into the designed room. Critics have traditionally placed this contrivance outside the realm of architecture, but we are now realizing it is deeply and centrally within that place. We make buildings to create interiors, and then deny this achievement, hiding it with façades and abstracting it into concerns about function.[10]

Architects have become more and more fascinated by the history of landscape. Instead of seeing buildings as autonomous appearances on the land, they understand them as part of the land that happens to coalesce or congeal into a solid structure. There is a romantic notion that agricultural buildings are no more than solidifications of the efforts to shape the land, and it is possible to view our cities in this way. If we consider the rivers, tectonic plates and soils on which our cities have risen, we begin to see the urban landscape as no more and no less than a tracing of that land.[11] Even our grandest structures maintain a relationship to the land. The architectural historian Vincent Scully was fond of comparing the cathedral of Chartres to the skyscrapers of Chicago and the silos of the American West, pointing out that they all celebrated (in their vertical stance) and stored converted form, though in the case of the cathedral paid for by the riches of the plains around the town, the wealth that the rolling wheat fields made possible.[12]

The interest in the vernacular, which asserted itself in architecture during the 1960s, has now extended to include the landscape.[13] Preservation movements care about agricultural legacies and parks as well as historically significant structures.[14] This means that we do not want new buildings to stand out in the landscape and the same has been true in the cityscape for quite some time (height limitations have long been implemented), giving

architects all the more reason to clothe their buildings with the mantle of nature. It has not always meant that buildings have respected the land (Frank Lloyd Wright is supposed to have said, "Doctors bury their mistakes, architects just plant ivy"), but it has made the integration of natural elements more attractive to designers.

In short, the tradition of landscapers offers an alternative history to the glorification of increasingly taller and more abstract edifices, producing a theory of the low, the folded and the hidden. Against the logical explanation of grids, structural systems and compositional relationships, the landscaper poses the unformed, unseen and almost unbuilt as a valuable condition. Thus, landscapers are as much part of a theoretical movement as they are a result of reasonable needs or societal attitudes.

A theory of landscapers opposes the idea of logical systems that we can use to construct rational structures with an unearthing of the hidden texts and textures of the world around us. It theorizes these two terms: the "texts" as latent structures that when read or edited always contain their original acts of signification; and the "textures" as continuous fields that we unfold to define ourselves as separate entities. It is not only the articulated differences among floor, ceiling and walls, or between columns and lintels that we consider to be the constituent elements of architecture. The cracks, fissures and faults in what we otherwise think of as the solid structure of the earth or ground allow a space of occupation to occur without assuming that it is necessarily different to the earth.

Similarly, the act of construction might not lead to the making of a structure that is fundamentally different from the world around it, but rather one that appears as if it is the refinement or revelation of the land. Just as a sculptor chisels away at a rock, the architect selects which strata to reveal, polishes them to change their appearance, and hones them down to show new

forms that were always inherent in the material itself. Architecture in this sense is not the making of something new, but the reformation of what already exists in a form that accepts the mark of human intervention. Thus, the making of landscapers is rather obtuse, dark and hidden. It assumes that everything around us is not only a physical appearance, but also a text or system of signification that we can understand by tracing its contours, unfolding its surface, or reading its textures. All we see is a ground, and all building could and should be a scraping of that ground to uncover readings—uses or experiences—from what already exists.

The foundations for this way of looking at the land on or out of which we build were laid by a group of mainly French and German thinkers in the 1960s. The approach swept American and European academies in the late 1980s through the teachings of Gilles Deleuze and Felix Guattari and the post-structuralists Jacques Derrida and Jean-François Lyotard. The rediscovery of major thinkers, including Martin Heidegger, Guy Debord and Henri Lefebvre, also played a part. These writers had quite different attitudes to the nature of land and how it should be converted by human constructions, but central to their thinking was the notion that the land should not be accepted as a given. Rather, it was an active text or texture that set the stage (the language or the site) for the work. The work (whether in words or in stones) should be considered as an attempt to elaborate, criticize or deform the land. Novels were a reformulation of language, just as buildings were reassemblies of building materials and forms, not new inventions. For architects this meant that their work was an unfolding of the text of the land.[15]

Derrida was not the oldest of these *penseurs*, but his influence was felt soonest and was the most pervasive. His long interest in architecture led him to several collaborations with such architects as Peter Eisenman, but his most direct influence was through his writing about the extension of textuality into texture. What to some might appear as a neutral carrier of meaning became a rich and fertile ground with its own reality for Derrida. Criticism was never something outside or on top of the text, he argued, so much as it was a re-reading, unfolding and "invagination" (as opposed to insemination) of the words and sentences. What seemed to be the new and the abstract was in fact no more than the allegorical expansion of what already existed.[16]

The implications of such thinking for architecture were obvious yet difficult to carry forward. How might one think of a building as an unfolding or an allegorical expansion, an invagination? Architects, such as Eisenman, played with abstract and textual ways of answering this question.[17] More and more designers, however, came to realize that they could see their buildings as re-weavings of existing materials and forms, and they sought to make visible the images that had always remained hidden within the buildings' closed forms. Critic Mark Wigley explored the theoretical value of this working method, emphasizing how it destabilized the idea of architecture as the building of rational structures on a neutral or abstract ground.[18] As Wigley (and several other critics working in Europe at the same time) pointed out, architects were always in the peculiar position of aspiring to the realization of abstraction as a way of making the perfect world envisioned by philosophers, while thereby burying their intentions in the base reality they sought to escape. Every time architecture tried to dissolve into "almost nothing," it buried its very nature in its foundations. So, there was always what Wigley called a "leaky, smelly crypt" hiding within the fabric of architecture, where, as architectural historian Anthony Vidler stated, some of the most fascinating writing on and experimentation in architecture took place. Here, the architect could make something that would not necessarily see the light of day, he or she could play with sexuality, exoticism and a sense of another reality without fear of its effects or inner contradictions.[19]

Lurking behind Derrida was the shadow of his sometimes acknowledged master Martin Heidegger. The Nazi thinker's essay "Building Dwelling Thinking"[20] has always been popular with certain architects, but post-structuralist criticism proposed other texts for architects' perusal. Seemingly obscure texts by Heidegger like *Early Greek Thinking*,[21] along with such major works as *Being and Time*,[22] encourage architects to think of their work as a "thoughtful gathering," a kind of "poetry." By this, Heidegger means that human labor should not merely be about the following or imposition of rules, but about a careful consideration of the purpose of our existence in the world. The land is important not just as a romantic agrarian ideal, but also as a witness to what is not human (ground) and what we do with that through the act of "gathering." This is the mark of human existence, setting us apart from the earth and establishing an alternative, artificial ground. All building can only be an elaboration of that original condition of emulation, establishment and essential separation.[23]

In his essay "The Question Concerning Technology," Heidegger contrasts the "challenging forth" of modern technology, which substitutes natural forms with human creations (for example, dams), with the gathering of form, image, intention, use and maker in the poetry of ancient works of art and architecture. He realizes that technology is bound to replace us as human beings and the earth we inhabit, but suggests that poetic activities allow us to "stand witness" to this disappearance in a way that would vouchsafe our humanity.[24]

In comparison to the Derridean and Heideggerian approach to unfolding the land, the writings of Guy Debord and Henri Lefebvre indicate a path more rooted in the artifacts of human civilization. Most well-known as the ringleader of the Situationist International,

PETER EISENMAN **WEXNER CENTER**

a group of avant-garde artists and left-wing political extremists,[25] Debord proposes that the human landscape is not only the field out of which new structures can appear, but also a collage of memories and experiences that need only be articulated or named to generate new forms. His patented method, the *dérive*—rapid wandering through the streets of Paris in an unplanned fashion, but involving playful and constructive behavior and an awareness of psychogeographical effects—traced the specifics of the urban condition.[26] Operating in much the same way as author Bruce Chatwin later described (or misread) the movements of Aborigines in *The Songlines*,[27] Debord sang alive the city with his uncovering of forgotten corners and his collage-like assembly of monuments that in reality were spaced far apart. The result was not so much the creation of a new city as it was a rediscovery of the city's inherent properties. It was an act of naming that gave significance to the very contour lines of daily existence.

It is interesting that the architectonic results of Debord's theories are large structures that seem to float over the earth. The "instant city" and "sin city" megastructures imagined by the Archigram group in England,[28] the ironic utopias of the Italian group Superstudio,[29] the neo-utopian structures created in France by Jean-Louis Chaneac and Antti Lovag[30] and Dutch artist Constant Nieuwenhuis's *New Babylon* (begun in 1974)[31] appeared to be self-sufficient systems. Yet, the architects all claimed that these structures were no more and no less than a gathering of the consumer goods, the technological systems that made these goods work, and the new ground of a growing capitalist city into a free-floating spectacle that architects and planners usually tried to hide with more traditional forms and restrictive grids. What the neo-situationists proposed was to formalize the ad hoc establishment of the landscapes that appeared out of almost unplanned development and the ones that appeared because people made use of the goods of a consumer society in

unpredictable ways (rock concerts and Times Square were favorites of the group) into self-sufficient structures. Situationist theory offered alternative views of the existing landscape as a labyrinth of endless choices, each one leading to another cluster of possible experiences. Whether these constructions were written, drawn, modeled or real mattered less than the fact that they were imagined. Architecture was not so much built work as possibilities unfolding in a dark cave, untouched and unburdened by the realities of gravity, construction or use that might turn them into fixed structures.

Theoretical development took place in the writings of Gilles Deleuze and Felix Guattari. Their first work, *Anti-Oedipus: Capitalism and Schizophrenia*[32] opposed the notion that madness and lesser forms of discomfort with reality were the result of a lack of control mechanisms within the psyche, as Sigmund Freud claimed, proposing instead that they arose from the same condition that constituted individual consciousness. The human being was the sedimentation of layers of consciousness and physical appearance whose identity emerged out of discontinuities with and inconsistencies in the fields of the body. Individuality was, to a certain extent, the same as madness; there was no "ground" even inside the human being on which to erect rational edifices. The unstable land, postulated as text by Derrida and experienced as a field of endless possibilities by the situationists, continued inside our heads.

In their magnum opus *A Thousand Plateaus: Capitalism and Schizophrenia*,[33] a sprawling accumulation of historical exegesis, philosophical theory and pseudo-scientific principles, Deleuze and Guattari developed these notions further. The work proposed an alternative system of organization, the rhizome, as a way of understanding physical and cultural forces. In parallel with Benoit Mandelbrot's[34] and Ilya Prigogine's[35] contemporaneous formulation of chaos theory, Deleuze and Guattari argued for non-hierarchical

structures without beginning and end, and often invisible.[36] Their model was the mushroom, which spreads into points of visibility from an underground network.

Deleuze and Guattari also supposed that culture was the appearance of complicated existing conditions as opposed to an alien imposition. They assumed that consciousness and human civilization were the results of the work of agents, whether the agents were the construction of the self (as opposed to others or the world) or nomads, coalescing paths and points into ways of thinking, or patterns of movement into settlements. These settlements became fixed, just as ways of thinking do, and patterns or forms emerged that became layered over time, and definitions between places became more rigid through ownership. Nomads became settlers, ways of looking and experiencing were turned into words, texts and eventually laws. The result was a complex landscape that merged human use and interpretation with what was left of the original ground to become what we now think of as a seamless landscape. This unity of thought, experience, place and pattern was termed "retroactive smoothing."[37] It was up to the new agents of change to cut through this smooth landscape to discover new patterns, to unfold the land to find its sedimentation and to open the mind to new ways of experiencing what it thought it already knew. Thus, retroactive smoothing made all complexity appear as a new ground that opened up and fissured into new "planes of consistency" or realities. If *A Thousand Plateaus* proposed anything, it was the unstable reality of these many strata, each of which formed a seemingly logical reality, but each of which was no more than a temporary unfolding of the universe through interpretation.[38]

In *Fold: Leibniz and the Baroque*,[39] Gilles Deleuze began to move toward an aesthetic theory of revelation within or through these plateaus. Acknowledging the eighteenth-century philosopher Leibniz, Deleuze suggested the "monad" as an

CONSTANT NIEUWENHUIS *NEW BABYLON*

alternative base unit of human consciousness and of mathematical consistency. This wandering moment of logic would exist at the intersection of planes, lines and moments in space and time. Baroque architecture, which sought to open up lines from the eye to the infinite, to connect interior enclosure and exterior elaboration, and to fuse clothing (texture), art and structure, might be the mode in which the monad could appear. Architecture would be a form of continuous unfolding of the existing strata of construction.

While Deleuze, Guattari and the situationists thought that a re-reading and elaboration of existing structures was the only possibility for architecture, Henri Lefebvre was calling for a more radical reconsideration of social construction. Lefebvre offered a thorough analysis of humanity through the medium of the land. Arguing that we know and construct ourselves through what he termed "socialized spatialities," Lefebvre reviewed social, political and economic conditions that were completely dependent on "the construction of space."[40]

According to Lefebvre, the first sense of what our society is or who we are is essentially spatial. One understands oneself (and here he follows Sartre[41]) as other than the world around us and like our fellow human beings. The sense of space is what makes us human beings with an interior and an exterior face, but it is also what removes us from the world. The exploration of the land we have gained (as an avenue of action) and lost (as now alien to us) marks the constitution, Lefebvre claims, of the social. The translation of land into territory, and the definition of such assigned space through legal and military means, becomes fixed in architecture as well as in language. The most elemental social relationships come from the continual contestation of such space.

Lefebvre goes on to define what he sees as the transformation of these tensions through ever-more-dense layers of representation in language and other forms of abstraction. The result of such layers of spatial assignment to various social practices is the city as we know it. Instead of understanding the built environment as a static fact, Lefebvre sees it as an accretion of millennia of appropriations and re-appropriations of land. What we experience, in other words, is a collection of forms, façades and spaces that are translations of endless negotiations expressed in property, in uses to which bits and pieces of land can be put, and in owners' desires to stake out their territory with walls and images that represent their identity. Not just the way buildings look, but their dimensions, proportions and materials fix, if only for a certain time, the complex economic, legal and social relationships that created them.[42] Our criticism of built space is no more than another layer on top of this social construction that takes meaning— this is good or bad, this costs so much—away from the structure and appropriates it for the critic or his or her reader. The structure is not stable, however, because those who are either removed from it or imprisoned by it continually attempt to take it over and make it their own—a struggle Lefebvre identifies as one of the most fundamental aspects of social relationships.[43]

Therefore, Lefebvre does not so much offer a proposal for building as call for a kind of archaeology that would begin to unearth the sedimented layers of our environment to free us from its heavy blankets. Lefebvre never calls for either direct social action or for the liberating possibilities of criticism, but he conceives a quasi-anarchic state in which all fixed and frozen relationships have been swept away and men and women live in an open community on a reclaimed land. Written at the height of Maoist infatuations in France, his conclusions sound like naïve evocations of an idyllic China, but they do offer a variation on the ever-upward thrust of construction in the opening up of social and spatial relationships.[44] The land, as that which constitutes the very essence of the social, must be revealed, and that is the ultimate work of the critic or any other cultural operator, such as an architect.

All of these tendencies seem to point to a secret history of architecture and an alternative future for the discipline. This history has parallels in literature and cultural criticism, as the notions of nomadic existence in the far past and the near future gain more prominence and we begin to realize that human and geological time are not that different and directly influence each other. One might even say that these theories seek to make sense of the way in which we have been making ourselves at home in the world within or outside the grand theories and structures proper to architecture. It seems that for centuries human beings have been carving out a place for themselves in structures that are either underground or barely visible. In many ways, this is the history of the repressed and the forgotten human beings, those without power who have had to hide in caves or grottoes. Perhaps it is no coincidence that Mao and his followers did so before they took over China, or that rebels retreat into the forest as Robin Hood did and modern-day guerrillas do. There they are invisible, building networks of minimal shelter that blend in with the ground, the trees and the bushes.

Invisible people are not always rebels; more commonly people hide in the ground because they do not have the means to express themselves. As the late and great historian of American landscape J. B. Jackson states, the only true vernacular is the sod hut or other structure that has no façade, no clear form and thus no way of presenting itself as part of a dominant culture.[45] It is anonymous and utilitarian, meaning that it is of the land. For many centuries a good percentage of the human population found itself in such anonymous structures: women had to make do with the interior, while men conquered territory. We wove together a realm out of the bits and pieces of nature, and later

GIOVANNI BATTISTA PIRANESI
*CARCERI* (THE DRAWBRIDGE)

we portrayed nature as a garden of delights or as a place of escape. The "feminine" in architecture, as our culture understands it, is a quality of place, land, the hidden and the sensual.[46]

The secret history of architecture is also one of communal spaces underground. From the earliest cult caves and the elaborate graves of pharaohs to the crypts in which early Christians hid from Roman authorities and to the fantastic realms Giovanni Battista Piranesi (1720–78) imagined, the underground has been a place where people came together to erect an alternative architecture and social structure. These fantastic constructions that isolate themselves from all outside form still survive today in our places of spectacle, where we sit in dark caverns to watch other lands unfold on the screen or stage.

Architectural historians have until recently found it hard to take such structures seriously, usually seeing them as obscure counterpoints to dominant architectural developments that were only of interest in so far as they achieved a moment or two of parity with the "magnificent play of forms in light" that was the proper domain of architecture.[47] Similarly, we as a culture do not speak freely of the delights of such spaces. They are either guilty pleasures or the secrets of our collective hearts.

Henri Lefebvre refers to these spaces as "representational," as opposed to "spaces of representation" imposed on us by dominant cultures.[48] Representational spaces are where we express ourselves, but as soon as they take a form that is recognizable to others they are immediately appropriated by the powers that be. They must remain secret and highly personal yet somehow shared. They must have the quality of allusion and elision, hinting at something we can feel or intuit, without ever clarifying themselves in the light of day. They are something we cannot define, except perhaps as poetry (as a technique) or as the making of what remains enigmatic: the forms and spaces pregnant with meaning that continually seduce us without ever making themselves clear.

To Michel Foucault, these spaces are "heterotopias" where time and space remain suspended as if in a mirror. Here, we are outside the normal flow of events in a space that is real and yet unreal. Foucault cites many examples in his now famous 1986 essay on the topic, and almost all are spaces that are dark, hidden or illusionary.[49] The heterotopia is not something that we would erect as a perfect place somewhere else or at some time in the future, but is a realizable alternative that exists in what we have already made if only we can find ways of unearthing it.

Many architects and designers have attempted to build such spaces. Raised on the teachings of Derrida, Debord, Lefebvre and Foucault, wary of the over-arching ambitions of their elders, and aware of the necessity to build with the land and not merely on it, they are drawing on the secret history of architecture to make a new kind of building: structures that are underground, on the ground, or barely above it. Their forms are not shaped by the niceties of classical or modernist styles, but rather mimic or respond to the specific site on which they are constructed. Torn from the earth or sinking into it, this is an architecture that is difficult to define, slipping away as it always does into the enigma of the earth.

Architects are unfolding the land in visionary and practical ways to find these representational, folded, rhizomatic and heterotopic spaces. Rather than preferring to build a utopian realm separate from nature or a "new Jerusalem" that would sit on a hilltop, some architects have been dreaming of buried and land-hugging structures. There is a history to this work, one that makes it central to the driving force of most good architecture: the experiments and dreams of which architects build only fragments.

Frank Lloyd Wright's Broadacre City (first conceived of in 1932), though often cited as the model for suburban sprawl, worked the land into a patchwork quilt of residences, cultural institutions, work places and infrastructure.[50] Even earlier, Italian Antonio Sant'Elia's 1914 visions of a Futurist architecture appeared like mountain ranges and canyons,[51] while New York–based architectural artist Hugh Ferriss made this tectonic nature of the modern city explicit in his The Metropolis of Tomorrow.[52]

These architects believed in the natural development of a new kind of man-made nature, which after World War II was taken to much further extremes by the members of Team x—the group who organized the tenth and last CIAM congress and went on to succeed CIAM—who proposed the integration of structure, services and function to produce continuous carpets of construction.[53] Paolo Soleri in the United States and members of the metabolist movement in Japan imagined structures in the form of spaceships that would remove themselves from the earth while attempting to replicate its characteristics. All that was built of such visions were a few "super slabs," such as Arthur Erickson's Simon Fraser University near Vancouver (Canada, 1963) and Shadrach Woods's Berlin Free University (Germany). Soleri's arcologies—a term coined from architecture and ecology—are another example, a series of high-density, fantastically unreal megastructures. The thirteenth arcology, Arcosani, has been under construction since 1970 in the desert north of Scottsdale, Arizona.

It was film makers, writers and artists who completed the architects' utopias. Building on the mixed utopian and dystopian visions of such films as Things to Come (William Cameron Menzies, 1936), Soylent Green (Richard Fleischer, 1973) and THX 1138 (George Lucas, 1970), and on such fiction as Thomas Pynchon's Gravity's Rainbow and Vineland, designers have begun to imagine a world underground.[54] Lebbeus Woods's 1988 series of images entitled Underground Berlin is

ANTONIO SANT'ELIA
**MONUMENTAL BUILDING**

ANTONIO SANT'ELIA
**POWER STATION**

PAOLO SOLERI **ARCOLOGY**

probably the most compelling. Picturing a world that may already exist in what were the then unused subway lines in the divided city, Woods drew a place inhabited by a society dedicated to producing knowledge about itself according to rules calibrated by the tectonic forces the people explored around themselves.[55]

As these types of spaces fill with activity, they break out of the ground. An architecture that is a fractured collection of the ruins of utopian dreams and an explosion of the rich but contained world of the cave is now rising up out of the earth. Its purpose is to re-write and re-right the uses of the land so that we understand the land and elaborate on it at the same time. It is a tortured yet exuberant architecture that seeks to reveal our origins, our base and our dreams of a new earth. The theories that led architects toward the land have obtained form here.

Architect Antoine Predock, who coined the phrase "landscrapers," defines his work as existing at the top of an imaginary road-cut (the cut builders make when they run roads and railroads through mountains) that reveals all geological history. Near the crown of the slice, strata of rocks give way to the accumulation of human history, from sod and timber to plastic and beer cans. Out of these layers an architecture unfolds in an attempt to be the organic outgrowth of human and geological history. It instates itself as an abstract, strange slice of construction pointing toward the sky. Responding to local conditions, but also defining itself as a line that moves away from the particular to something that is wholly human in its artifice, architecture poses as a question that cannot be answered except through our experience of the structure.

The end point of such an architecture might be the shaping of the land itself. Land artists of the 1960s and 1970s pointed the way toward a reduction of human marks in or on the land. This is the "sculpture in the expanded field" of which Rosalind Krauss

spoke in 1979.[56] The pure abstraction of such pieces makes us aware of the relationship between the land and our own construction. We experience a tension between what we know through our rational senses and what we feel is present on a site. Such "deep knowledge" might make us keener to preserve the land, but it might also make us understand the artificiality of our endeavors to make something out of that land. Finally, we might become aware that our own upright posture and all that flows from our exploration and exploitation of the land is what constitutes us as human beings and alienates us from the world.

If we reduce even further our attempt at awareness of who we are as human beings in relation to the land, we also come to the shaping of the land. To understand such a Mecca of architecture as Chicago, one should consider the small garden landscape architect Dan Kiley created in front of the south wing of the Chicago Art Institute (1962). A few feet below street level, surrounded by orthogonal boxes that thrust up to the sky in celebration of human achievement and measured by a grid of trees that recalls the simple clarity with which we organize the land to make such ambitious construction possible, this small garden is the essence of what we build on the land.

Many landscape architects today see their practices as a way of unearthing and clarifying what already exists. They follow the contours of the land, molding it only to make it clearer, reconstructing wetlands and implementing remediation plans for brownfield sites. Their designs make us aware of what we did to the land as we restore it; they combine human shaping with the force of the land. Landscape architecture that exists at the intersection of the geological, the geographical and the human is the most fundamental exposition of architecture I know.

Perhaps it is because I grew up and now again live in the Netherlands that such approaches make sense to me. "God made the world, but the Dutch made Holland," reads an ancient proverb,

and this is largely true. Most of what is known as the Netherlands would be under water if it were not for the elaborate reclamation projects in which the Dutch have engaged since the early Middle Ages. The efforts to collectively reclaim and form the land gave birth to the particular nature of Dutch society, but it has also shaped every aspect of the environment. This essentially flat land reveals itself as a grid of polders, drainage ditches and dykes out of which the three-dimensional structures of human inhabitation grow. Very few things have, until recently, risen much above sea level. The absolute artifice of the land is clear in the land itself.

This book is an attempt to find such clarity in a catalog of recent structures. Landscrapers are buildings that make us aware of who we are by where we are on the land. They take many forms, but in all cases they unfold the land, promising to lay a new ground on which we can erect an architecture of the land.

ANTOINE PREDOCK **SPENCER THEATER**

**1**
**Engineered Utopias**
The material and physical act of shaping the earth through technology and innovation has opened up a realm of ideals

**2**
**Caves and Caverns**
Burrowing into the land to discover new spatial experiences

**3**
**Unfolding the Land**
Opening up the earth to create architectural forms

**4**
**A New Nature**
Buildings that merge landscape with architecture, the natural with the human

# 1
## Engineered Utopias

The material and physical act of shaping the earth through technology and innovation has opened up a realm of ideals

HOOVER DAM       LE CORBUSIER **PLAN OBUS FOR ALGIERS**

The impulse behind the creation of an earthbound form, or landscraper, is often to reveal the hidden and turn it into architecture. However, the architecture of landscrapers usually appears as something rather more bold: a direct challenge to nature. If the theoretical underpinnings of the landscraper lie in a reading of the land, its practical roots appear in making the land right for habitation or agriculture. For centuries, engineers have been making practical landscrapers: dams, dykes and defensive bulwarks intended to alter the contours of the land. Embedded in the most basic defensive structures at the heart of architecture, such forms have long offered a vision of the immensely large, the abstract and the perfect in a world of forms whose complexity comes from the contingencies of human occupation. In the twentieth century, architects engaged in one of their most ambitious projects of all time: to turn works of engineering into places of occupation. The resulting fragments of a new nature took on a utopian character and the megastructures proposed a new form of living not so much on the land, as in a new land.

In the pre-modern period the line between such engineering feats and architecture was not absolute, and most architects who trained in northern Europe still received engineering degrees. From this viewpoint, architecture was no more than a subset of the manipulation of material to respond to natural conditions and the need—either for shelter or defense—for interiors. It was only as the French system of architecture as the articulation of culture in built form gained dominance that engineering was removed from the purview of architects and placed squarely in the realm of science.[1] How things were made was allied with nature, and how they appeared on top of nature became the realm of art, culture and architecture.[2]

In the twentieth century, more and more people became aware of the achievements of engineering. As bridges and towers became larger and bolder, the act of construction itself became evident. As subways were built, people other than miners inhabited the carefully shored-up caves that coursed below the ground. As human beings began to control water not just in sewage systems and aqueducts, but by erecting vast dams and other structures to displace and move water, the power of such gestures became apparent.[3]

Thus, when the subways of London and Paris were constructed in the second half of the nineteenth century, new sets of spaces emerged that had their foundation in caves, but behaved like recognizable urban constructs. Urban dwellers became familiar with the underground; the subway's tubular shapes, frightening labyrinthine nature and darkness were negotiated daily by commuters. It was an intensification of what the city above had become, a dark and unknowable place, filled with motion and continually pressing in on us. It was only during the twentieth century that subways, such as the one in Washington, D.C. (ironically based on Stalin's great monuments to totalitarian retreat in Moscow and St Petersburg), became places of seeming order and rationality, covered with the coffered vaults that mimic the temples of democratic government above their hidden corpses.

In science fiction, the subway has become the model abode for a future society when the earth's surface is no longer habitable. Whether it is a race of engineers building a new world after the destruction of war in the stylish film *Things to Come* (William Cameron Menzies, 1936), or the prophetic beehive of isolated cells imagined by E.M. Forster in his 1908 novella *The Machine Stops*,[4] these works and others like them assumed that the underground was our destiny. As if in preparation for this actually happening, citizens of the United States and the Soviet Union in the 1950s and 1960s built entire underground cities for themselves. Fear, combined with a desire to use technology to escape any sense of bodily reality, has led to the proliferation of underground passages from Tokyo to Houston. More frightening, more and more interiors—offices, shopping malls or places of entertainment—are underground without us even noticing. The true architecture of the underground might be the banal coffin of fluorescent-lit normality in which we find ourselves imprisoned.

While many of us occupy the underground world out of which we thought we had escaped, others have come to confront the ways in which we shape the land. Here, again, engineers have shown us the way. The massive dams and dykes that now control so much of the world's water supply are heroic in their scale, towering above us while radically altering the natural environment over vast territories. The Hoover Dam (finished in 1934, opened in 1940) is one of the wonders of the world that is visible from space, while the Three Gorges Dam, now nearing completion in China, will displace millions of people. There is a beauty to such structures in their sheer scale and in the way they abstract or stand in opposition to the natural contours of the land.

The same is true of certain road and railroad structures, which twist and wind their way through tortuous terrain or graze the tops of unstable or marshy soil. Here, the pure line of engineering stands in stark contrast to nature, expressing movement yet creating a barrier within the landscape. The most beautiful evocation of the power of roads and dams is Le Corbusier's Plan Obus for Algiers (1932), a long and sinuous snake of continuous habitation that unfurls along the coastal ridges of Algeria. Although the project was never constructed, the idea of roads (and the terraces of land below and above them) as inhabitable structures at a vast scale haunts the imagination of architects, whether in the schemes of Archigram from the 1960s or those of Cesar Pelli in the 1970s.[5]

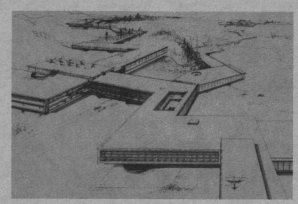

CONSTANT NIEUWENHUIS *NEW BABYLON*

The immense aircraft carriers that emerged from the Second World War became the model for dreams of itinerant and very large communities, providing landscapers that were completely divorced from the land. Much larger than any other structure that had ridden the waves, the "floating cities" were nothing more or less than a flat surface from which airplanes could be deployed. To support this activity, however, the navy needed to build what amounted to a complete urban structure. The final shape was a strange hybrid: a piece of flat land, a stubby control tower, a base whose inverted v-shape was the opposite of the forms we expect to result from the laws of gravity, and a complex and densely packed layer cake of functions with stray pieces bulging out here and there. The aircraft carrier became a favorite model for such architects as Hans Hollein, but also served as a logical counter to the kinds of sculptural explorations generated by the end of the Second World War.[6] The balance of horizontal and vertical stripes in a gravity-defying composition marks the paintings of Franz Kline and Robert Motherwell, while the breakdown of a composed picture in favor of an overall field is evident in Jackson Pollock's drip paintings.

Perhaps the inspiration for postwar earthbound forms was more immediate, however. The need for housing led to the spread of suburban nodes grouped around urban cores into a carpet of forms that hugged the land more closely. While some architects, such as Quincy Jones in Los Angeles, proposed burying the suburban home in the ground, the reality was a loose system of identical parts across the land. If anything was responsible for architects of the 1950s and 1960s making landscrapers, it was their desire to make sense—coherent form—out of the sprawling mess. Their model wavered between Frank Lloyd Wright's Broadacre City and Le Corbusier's Plan Obus for Algiers, between a vague collection of disparate and discreet pieces and the amalgamation of functions into the single form of an escarpment carved by circulation, sunlight and other natural conditions. The outcome was the disappearance of modestly scaled, isolated buildings as the basic unit of architectural vision. Postwar architects, faced with the destruction of much of Europe, the possibility of transforming the Third World according to rational, industrial principles, and the ever-grander dreams of the United States, articulated a vision of architecture dissolving into a form of planning. Architecture was no longer to be the making of isolated objects decreed the members of CIAM (Congrès Internationaux d'Architecture Moderne, an international collective of the self-appointed architectural avant-garde), but was the rational organization of all forms of land use.[7]

Endless blocks of flats, office buildings and unidentifiable fragments of three-dimensional grids were the most visible results of this attitude and the reality of economic conditions. It was a grim time for architecture that gave shape to the land or responded to the human body. Architecture became what folk singer Malvina Reynolds called the creation of "little boxes" that appeared without regard to the land, were identical, isolated themselves from natural conditions with electric light, televisions, and air conditioning, and sometimes assembled themselves into the face- and place-less grids made famous in such films as *Playtime* (Jacques Tati, 1968) and *Alphaville* (Jean-Luc Godard, 1965). Ironically, it was in the hands of the most radical and megalomaniacal designers that this strategy cohered into the "flat heroic," a freer and more human-centered form of design.

Alison and Peter Smithson, leaders of the Team X group that succeeded CIAM and proposed the flat heroic, led the way with such projects as Golden Lane Housing in 1952, which assembled housing blocks into sinuous horizontal lines stacked on top of each other while tracing existing footpaths.[8] Also, Dutch firm Van den Broek & Bakema suggested melding housing, shopping and offices into a carpet of interlocking squares that covered the devastated heart of Rotterdam in their Lijnbaan Center (1945–53).

By the mid-1960s, architects were developing coherent forms (according to the local environment) that would break with the anonymity of housing and office blocks. They wanted to mine the massiveness of this development mandated by an economy growing at a rapid pace and a technology tying more and more of the world together. Mastaba-like mounds rose up from contours that conformed to existing conditions. They were carved to receive sunlight while minimizing shadows, used the need for internal communication to create dense connective tissues of ramps, stairs and walkways, and contained communal caves for theaters, community centers or sports centers.

The most thoroughly shown earthbound project of the post-Second World War era was Dutch artist Constant Nieuwenhuis's *New Babylon*. Assembled from paintings, drawings and models over the course of three decades, *New Babylon* proposes a utopian community given over to pleasure. Nieuwenhuis allied himself with Situationist International, founded by Guy Debord in 1957, believing in the necessity of play and discovery as a central organizing principle in modern life. If it was true that technology could set us free, these artists argued, we should not reproduce its enabling principles in the forms we are now able to explore.[9] If work was becoming more and more rational and taking up less and less time, and production was minimized, what would we do with all the free time and space? Use it to wander without limit, explore the land, our bodies and each other, they suggested.

PAOLO SOLERI **ARCOLOGY**

*New Babylon's* plastic models and neo-expressionist paintings depicted a completely new ground plane, an artificial landscape that would hover over the earth while keeping its inhabitants protected from sun and rain. The structure took the implication of Le Corbusier's *villes pilotis* (1915), seeking to remove humanity from its polluted and dangerous daily life into a realm of perfected modernity, to the extent of creating a reality whose occupants would never have to come into contact with the earth. The topography of hills and dales would be reproduced in a geometric form, while nature would be shown as an artificial garden. Within the layers of *New Babylon*, Nieuwenhuis proposed an open web of caves that would have the complexity of Piranesi's prisons, but that would be open and joyous.[10]

Nieuwenhuis's aspirations found a parallel in Kenzo Tange's so-called metabolist dreams for Tokyo Bay (1960) and eventually in the communal hives Paolo Soleri termed "arcologies." A small fragment of the latter is under construction in the Arizona desert, where its rough concrete arches and stepping stones of housing and offices combine the rational spread of form, the engineer's aesthetic of large structural gestures, and the history of land-mimicking forms of the local Anasazi and Pueblo people. Thereby, the essential contradiction inherent in the flat heroic is illustrated: the desire to make an open structure and the vision of a consistent new nature. This formal tension mirrors contrasting social tendencies toward, on the one hand, democratic openness and, on the other hand, controlled and cohesive social structures.

Projects thus veered between the amalgamation of functions into constructions large and grand enough to reflect the natural setting, and carpets of intersecting rectangles that imitated and intensified the agricultural purpose of the landscape. The geometric carpet, which reached its clearest expression in Shadrach Woods's Berlin Free University

(1963–73), was supported by the then fashionable notion of "field theory," in which the appearance and destiny of an object, whether a rock or (by implication) a human being, was determined by the conditions in the field out of which it emerged.[11] Woods and others proposed an open-ended and adaptable grid that would mimic a democratic political system, so that whatever was produced by the field would be as open and unpredictable as possible. For administrators or clients, the strategy promised infinite flexibility in the allocation of spatial resources and expansibility, assuming a new landscape that would be completely neutral.

Conversely, the makers of monoliths usually gave a sense of place to the emerging institutions of the postwar era, with examples of such megastructures hugging the land all over the developed world. Three of the most notable were Patrick Hodgkinson's Brunswick Centre (1959–72), a set of slabs with sloping façades that faced each other in the heart of London's Bloomsbury district, Arthur Erickson's Simon Fraser University near Vancouver (Canada, 1965) and his later Robson Square Government Center (1978–83) in the same city. By placing Simon Fraser University along a ridge overlooking the city, Erickson made it into an isolated world. The complex was one large rectangular concrete box of ranks of offices and classrooms. Auditoriums and meeting places cut through the march of rational form, and the whole presented itself as a giant form overriding incidents of topography to proclaim the victory of a new kind of place. However, unlike skyscrapers, which were the expression of individual or corporate power, these were sprawling representations of the people's (or their delegate, the state's) ability to make a new world. The most extreme example of this new world is Agustin Hernandez's National Military Academy (1975–78). Outside Mexico City, the academy's ritualistic mounds compete with those of the Aztec culture.

Three giant mastabas house dormitories, while administrative areas rise out of the earth like over-scaled antitank guards, and the stables and cavalry yards are concentric circles incised into the earth. Because of its size and menacing, cantilevered and sharp forms, there is a sense of complete and terrible beauty about the structure that seeks to inculcate the absolute fact of the central state into young recruits. Ironically, these forms most frequently occur in the design of massive seaside resorts from Cancun, Mexico to southern Spain.

Buildings that make a total and integrated new nature (also evident, in a milder form, in such structures as the United States Air Force Academy in Colorado Springs, designed by Gordon Bunshaft, 1956–62) become an expression of central bureaucracy, a state that lost favor in the 1960s and only survives today in science-fiction movies. The optimistic belief in creating institutions that would be as grand and logical as nature became a vision of a totalitarian state that would subject everybody to its rules and quite literally bury them in such movies as *Lost Horizon* (Frank Capra, 1937). In several of the movies designed by Ken Adams, including *Dr. Strangelove: Or How I Learned to Stop Worrying and Love the Bomb* (Stanley Kubrick, 1963) and the early James Bond movies *Goldfinger* (Guy Hamilton, 1964) and *Doctor No* (Terence Young, 1962), communal mounds were the lairs of evil powers who commanded vast forces that they sent out from their concealed complexes to conquer the world.[12]

Other than the Berlin Free University and the many less successful and mainly educational and hospital structures it inspired, the contrasting tendency toward open fields at first seemed to be marginalized. The British collective Archigram, however, presented a more joyful and open version of an integrated new nature. Starting in 1962 and drawing on disparate influences, which included the Japanese Metabolist

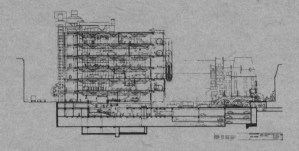

RENZO PIANO AND RICHARD ROGERS **CENTRE POMPIDOU**

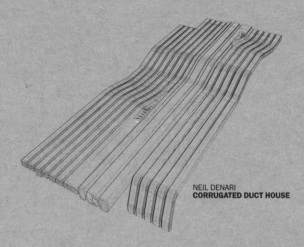

NEIL DENARI
**CORRUGATED DUCT HOUSE**

visions of massive new cities and the science-fiction imagery of space-age urbanity, a small band of young architects began to develop an architecture that responded to the increasingly loose and mobile nature of Western democracy. Plug-In City (1964–66), for instance, a project instigated by Peter Cook at Archigram, proposed that cities should be organic structures that grew like spores: small pods, connected by a grid of services without a clear center or origin, could pop up wherever they were required. Inhabitants would be free to plug in whatever appliances they needed, even living and sleeping modules. The city would dissolve into this amorphous carpet that would have a loose enough weave to allow for individual expression and an experience of existing conditions, whether rural or urban. The landscraper would not be a closed behemoth, rather a structure continually redefining and reforming itself.[13]

The Centre Pompidou, designed by Archigram disciples Richard Rogers and Renzo Piano and finished in 1977, was in many ways a version of this vision, which the British High-Tech movement then turned into the regularized world of giant airports and corporate headquarters. However, few of these buildings were ever truly completed, coalescing once again into massive structures. Airports are the most notable, of which the most successful is Renzo Piano's Kansai Airport outside Osaka in Japan (1988–94). Built on an artificial island, the mile-long structure is an abstract wave undulating on its reclaimed plot in a mixed metaphor of images of airplane wings and water movement. The huge spaces sheltered by the envelope are open and animated by the users (though not as much as the architect's renderings would have us believe), and our experience of them is intended to liberate us from our earthbound concerns and prepare us for flight. In these buildings, the sculptural

implication of the modern mastaba makers meets the dreams of an open, technologically fed future as envisioned by members of Archigram.

Not all the work of high-tech gurus has disappeared into the creation of structures for mobility. Rogers and Foster and their associates and followers, such as Nicholas Grimshaw and William Alsop, continue to practice an architecture of the large, the organic and the utopian in the deformed modes that seem proper to times in which nature can take any form at the click of a computer mouse. Of all of the members of this—mainly British—movement, Lord Foster is the most restrained. His vast cushion of steel and glass, the Great Glass House at the National Botanic Garden of Wales in Carmarthenshire (1995–2000, see p. 32) approaches the utopian ideals implicit in his use of technology. Its modest entrance reveals a world of eroding cliffs and striated fields designed by landscape artist Kathryn Gustafson. Huge and undifferentiated except by nature, Foster's form is a mere napkin of architecture thrown over a contrived version of nature.

While the reality of financing and codes has meant that Rogers's buildings are considerably more static and monumental than he had hoped (helped by the fact he incorporates a sense of the fixed, the grand and the memorable in such buildings as the Law Courts in Bordeaux, 1999), he has continued to dream of an architecture in which technology would open us to nature. In 1998, he proposed a plan for central London, consisting of bridges, walkways, and skyscrapers. Fragments of high technology, they would draw the city together while gaining their energy from sun and water. Somewhere between trees or shrubs and the exposed interiors of power plants, these structures would make Londoners aware of the energy that keeps their city going and the essential characteristics of a landscape long buried by the boxy forms of urban living.[14]

On a much smaller scale, Future Systems' House in Wales (1998, see p. 26) more clearly establishes a new space. It is a direct outgrowth of the Doughnut House the studio designed in 1986 as an experiment to create a submerged, torus-shaped building reached by a short tunnel. The new house opens up on one side to the view, but both houses share a stressed skin, although in the built version it is made out of aluminum rather than fabric. The built work is a perfect bubble emerging out of the landscape, its pure form standing in contrast to the flowing forms of the land around it. The architects have worked with the local geology and produced a machine that does not so much sit in the "garden" as it comes out of that natural setting.

Los Angeles architect Neil Denari has created a land-scraper that exposes technology while following the contours of the land. His Corrugated Duct House in Palm Springs, California (1997–98, see p. 28) presents a row of parallel tubes to the outside world, forming a thick roof filled with water that insulates the house from the desert sun. The house sinks into the ground, reducing cooling costs, and finally flows into a backyard pool sheltered by the surrounding landscape. Denari has designed a loftlike modernist environment that does away with the bravura of standing against the landscape and instead slithers close to the ground like the seductive snake of technology.

Utopian landscrapers have tended to incorporate ideas about the environment in recent years. They have also fragmented into smaller and more tentative forms, open-ended systems that attempt to restore the ecosystem. Japanese architect Shuhei Endo, for example, creates the building blocks for utopia with simple materials. He has developed a patented method of bending corrugated steel plates into continuously unraveling cones, which he places in parallel strips on the

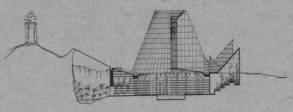

EMILIO AMBASZ **LUCILLE HALSELL CONSERVATORY**

MICHAEL SORKIN **UTOPIAN PROJECT**

landscape. Programmatic spaces, supported by steel planes, weave in and out of the continuous ribbon. Endo calls it "Springtecture," and has applied it to various sites from public lavatories to a museum (see p. 34). The effect is one of playful curves whose repeated rhythms give a feeling of order that is light and open-ended, rather than closed and massive.

The master of utopian landscraper fragments is Argentinian-born, New York–based architect Emilio Ambasz. In 1984, Ambasz suggested an underground house as a garden folly. Instead of proposing an object in the field, he created a place of retreat sheltered by the garden itself. His interest in underground buildings continued through the 1980s, and led to the construction of the Lucille Halsell Conservatory in San Antonio's botanical gardens, Texas (1988). A set of conical skylights is the only evidence above ground of the extensive spread of gardens that are paradoxically underground. The earth is used as a container, protector and insulator of plant life. The curving glass forms imitate the contours of the site while leading visitors along paths that are reminiscent of an English garden in their winding paths, controlled vistas and carefully composed plantings. What is inside and what is outside, what is garden and what is building?

As Ambasz has developed his forms they have become their own pieces of landscape. He has designed buildings as natural disturbances in the landscape. Instead of earthquakes or glaciers throwing up these volumes toward the skies, it is the program and construction that produce the novel but barely visible form in the landscape. At their best, the buildings have the character of what Adolf Loos once called the only "authentic" architecture: a grave marker found in the forest. Without pretense to the imposition of outside orders that makes a façade or mass appear in what society might regard as the correct manner, Ambasz's buildings are free to develop—as

the land might—in slow, rising curves, moments of upthrust, valleys and depressions. Inside, shards and waves of glass open up a new realm where nature or the sky fill the view.[15]

The most successful of Ambasz's built work is the Fukuoka Prefectural International Hall in Japan (1995–99, see p. 48). A small plaza rises up into a set of terraces planted with a variety of trees, bushes and plants, and as the visitor crisscrosses the ascending ledges on ramps, water courses down rills and waterfalls. Before visitors have become aware of it, they are standing twenty stories above the ground on top of a large office building. Planes of glass interrupt views on the way to the top, so visitors are suddenly confronted with a vertiginous view down into the building's central atrium. While the hall presents a reserved face to the city on three sides, the fourth side confuses the difference between open space and building, garden and landscape.

Such an involution (if not to say convolution) reaches Rococo levels of intensity in the utopian proposals by designer Michael Sorkin (see p. 40). Long a believer in an "organic" architecture, Sorkin suggests small communities that take the idea of the old "garden suburb" (small isolated communities close to nature but made possible by technology) one step further. His little villages, sized to enable everybody to have a personal relationship with everybody else, spread out across the landscape and are formed from the contours of the land, gathering together in tightening spirals to provide homes. Recycling, solar collecting, and waste-water re-use almost make the communities self-sufficient, while the most up-to-date technology keeps them plugged into the global economy and culture.

What is most remarkable about the settlements is the totality of Sorkin's vision: curves and circles dominate every aspect, from the shape of the overall communities to the walls

of every house. In an attempt to be as natural as nature, Sorkin has designed a world where complexities have a decorative quality, as if they are trying to formalize nature's rules without translation into the artifices of human habitation.[16]

Sorkin's utopian projects owe something to Ernest Callenbach's 1975 novel *Ecotopia*,[17] an influential book that imagines a Pacific Northwest that has seceded from the rest of the United States. It is a self-sufficient, fiercely independent state where cars are banned, energy comes from such re-use and replenishable resources as the sun and water, and governance is a ground-up affair. As envisioned in a series of designs for a film version of the novel, architect and urban scenarist Craig Hodgetts's *Ecotopia* would be a place where skyscrapers sprout plants of all sorts, cable cars span space, and technology and nature become totally intertwined. In contrast to the tendency to bury space, Hodgetts harks back to the optimism of Stewart Brand's 1960s hippy manual, *Whole Earth Catalogue*. Technology and plants grow and develop together into forms that move away from a tradition of orthogonal shapes, defensive walls and sharp differences between inside and outside. Green architecture makes a truly organic network of skeletons that start out as human inventions and continue as plants, for example, walls that dissolve into nature, and spaces that flow not in a mimicry of topography but because technology has reduced the barriers between the natural and the artificial into almost nothing.[18]

The largest contributions toward a utopian architecture, however, come from designers who work directly with the landscape without trying to make enclosed forms. A new generation of landscape architects is redefining and restoring the land to a state where its common enjoyment draws us together in public spaces and makes us conscious of where we are. While architects continue to wrestle with how to make

LAWRENCE HALPRIN **THE SEA RANCH COMMUNITY**

ALEXANDRE CHEMETOFF
**PARC DE LA VILLETTE**

HARGREAVES ASSOCIATES **CRISSY FIELDS**

buildings—camouflaging, breaking down, burying and hiding their otherwise so proud and isolated creations—landscape architects reclaim the primacy of the land as a shaper of communal experience. They do so because they do not take responsibility for how we live and work, rather they provide a new ground on which others might imagine building.[19]

Such was certainly the case when Lawrence Halprin envisaged The Sea Ranch Community on Northern California's Sonoma Coast in 1962. Along fifteen miles of Pacific coast, he planned rows of homes that would follow the fall of the bluffs toward the ocean. Parallel lines of trees and hedges would act as windbreaks, roads to the houses, and rhythmic divisions along the long stretch of coast. Halprin was not necessarily restoring the original landscape, but he was using the vernacular of agricultural land patterns to make us aware of the site's contours. The zoning regulations he devised with architectural firm MLTW (Charles Moore, Donlyn Lyndon, William Turnbull and Richard Whitaker) forced designers to trace the contours of the land, building with the earth rather than on it. The buildings, therefore, expend a minimal amount of energy because they defer to land, water and wind instead of attempting to resist them.[20]

Revealing what lies repressed in the ground is a strong element in landscape architecture. Alexandre Chemetoff's design for the Bamboo Garden, an underground garden at Parc de la Villette in Paris (1990), allows visitors to descend below ground level and to wander through bamboo forests while the sewage pipes that are usually buried underground run above their heads. Human infrastructure and artificial nature mingle to conjure up exotic fantasies that lie hidden in the city's history. Kathryn Gustafson, Chemetoff's former employee, prefers sweeping gestures in which grass covers vast expanses of building. Defining the difference between building

and landscape, she states, "If there's sky, it's mine," and proceeds to increase her palette as much as possible. In the National Botanic Garden of Wales (see p. 32), the nearly invisible skin hovers over an elaborate journey through the topographies and floral patterns of the world, cut into the limestone cliffs. Without a solid horizon line, this building or garden is excavation and roof, but nothing else.

On a more formal note, landscape architect Bernard Lassus abstracts and fragments classical traditions to integrate them into the urban environment. His design for Le Parc de la Corderie Royale in Rochefort-sur-Mer (1988) houses community services within old naval installations, balancing the starkness of the building with the abstract tree plantings and allées. Lassus has continued to rescue a sense of grandeur from the remains of an industrial past with such grand projects as the Parc André Citroën in Paris (1997).

German designer Peter Latz marries industry and nature in his designs for Landscape Park Duisburg Nord in the Ruhr Valley. His gradual reclamation of one of the huge steel plants, which once made the valley Europe's industrial heartland, has been progressing since the beginning of the 1990s with the emptying out, cleaning up and reoccupation of the industrial buildings. Latz has left many of the forms standing in the landscape, for example, the castle ruins that remind visitors of the glories of a past civilization (and of the impermanence of their own achievements). A set of interconnected outdoor spaces weave through the ruins: secret gardens hidden in roofless sheds, walkways that follow the site's contours, and theaters carved out of the former wasteland. These spaces are hybrids of nature and the man-made, of the useful and the useless, of the enclosed and the open. The resulting landscaper is so much part of the land or site that it is difficult to distinguish from the original condition.

In the United States, landscape architect Julie Bargmann of D.I.R.T. Studio works with disused industrial sites. Carving with a big digger rather than a shovel, Bargmann moves vast amounts of earth to accentuate and restore river beds, wetlands and other features of the natural terrain. An open pit mine becomes a potential piece of sculpture by the reshaping of its contours. In a former coal-mining town in West Virginia, she has built a park that reclaims the discarded sludge or "tailings" from the mine. Colors and forms of plantings resemble and trace the spread of the toxic minerals across the landscape, providing an aesthetic enjoyment that comes with an understanding of what so violently reshaped the piece of land.

In George Hargreaves's opinion, we often dismiss or suppress the forces of wind and water that shape the contours of the land. His work often consists of reintroducing their effects by restoring wetlands, watersheds and natural contours. While his early projects, such as Candlestick Cultural Park in San Francisco (1988), have an overtly sculptural quality, in recent years he has made forms out of, rather than on, the landscape. In San José, Hargreaves has been working to re-form the Guadalupe River Park since 1994 (see p. 30). Unearthing the seasonal stream from underneath the concrete corset the U.S. Army Corps of Engineers had laid over it, he has designed a meandering park coursing along the edge of downtown. Various episodes along the way make the river into an object of use: one bend in the river becomes an outdoor amphitheater, the meeting place with a stream is an outlook, a straight course leads to an open field. The design stitches back together nature, the city and human enjoyment of the land.

In his designs for Crissy Fields in San Francisco, Hargreaves has concentrated on restoring the area's history. Wetlands are present once again, where water and land mix and native grasses grow. The fall of the land toward the bay, the spread of the ground as it builds up through deposits, and the rough edges where water defines the boundaries are again visible. At the heart of the project, however, stands a piece of human history: what was the city's original airfield is now a vast plane of grass. Swept by the same wind that sent planes aloft, the open arena is a place for free play, sunbathing and the enjoyment of so much open space in a crowded city. It is a geometric solid that is not the base for building, but rather a site for understanding what we do in our quest for solid, permanent form, and what nature makes and remakes every moment of every day.

Landscape architecture today is not simply about planting flowers and creating outdoor spaces with plants. In the hands of such designers as Hargreaves, Gustafson and many others it is the act of scraping off the products of human interference on the land to reveal the nature of a place. They find and exhibit the geology, topography and hydrology of the land along with the layers of human intervention that also shape the ground on which we live and build, producing a history of design transformations that change over time and in relation to natural forces. This is the most efficient and at the same time the most utopian form of architecture as the engineering of the land: one that does not try to hide habitation or to do as little harm as possible, but one that restores nature and our understanding of it to a prominent position in our culture.

The future peeks out from the seaside cliffs of Wales in this small house designed by the purveyors of realizable science fiction. Adapted from an early scheme for an all-metal, ovoid residence that hovered over the landscape, a stressed-plywood roof stretches between two hillocks. The architects covered the roof with sod, leaving only a small, eye-shaped glass wall to peer out to sea. The natural and the new ground covering the residence allow a near-constant temperature to be maintained, while the glass wall makes the visual virtues of the site all the more apparent.

*opposite* front façade I *far left* aerial view I *left* view of roof I *below left* view from the beach I *below* model

## FUTURE SYSTEMS
## HOUSE IN WALES

# NEIL DENARI
# CORRUGATED DUCT HOUSE

Making monumental form out of what is usually the hidden guts of a house, Neil Denari proposed burying the 2,000-square-foot (186-square-meter) house in Palm Springs, CA under an undulating roof of oversized corrugations. Eight-inch (20cm) steel sections form hexagonal tubes that span the flexible interior and through which water and air move to cool the house below. The inside, the surfaces of which are as slick and manufactured as the roof, becomes a stepped cave that opens up to a backyard pool.

*left* duct detail | *below left* view from back across pool

*below* front aerial view | *opposite, top* elevation

*opposite, middle and bottom* long sections

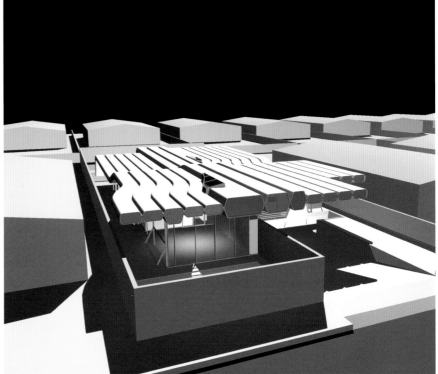

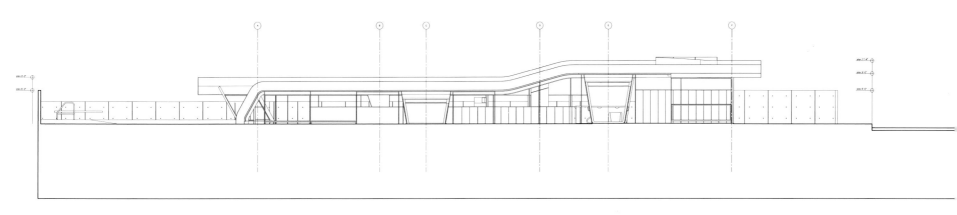

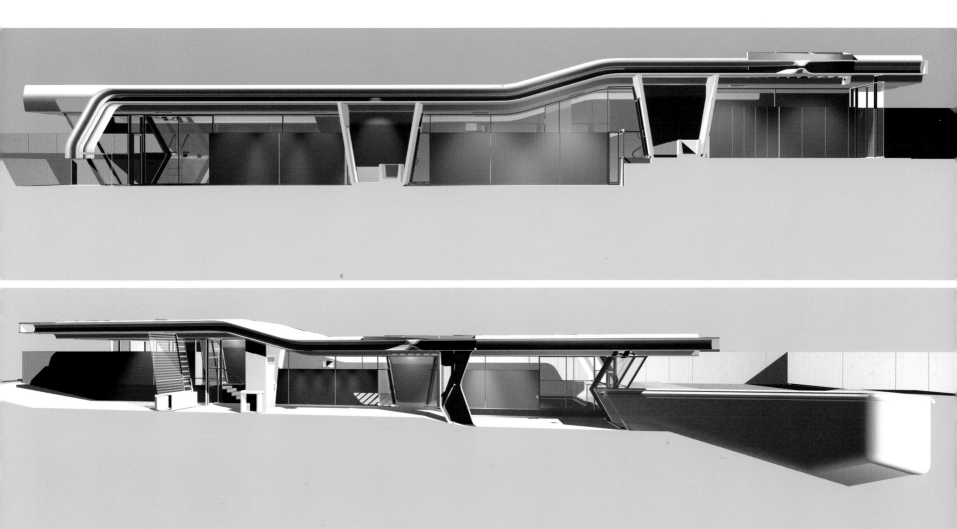

# HARGREAVES ASSOCIATES
## GUADALUPE RIVER PARK

George Hargreaves's project of ecological revitalization reveals the buried landscape of the San Francisco peninsula. This 3-mile (5km) stretch along the Guadalupe River had for many years been a flood-control channel designed by the u.s. Army Corps of Engineers. Hargreaves is turning it into a linear park that retains the flood-control measures, cutting through the center of San José's downtown and leading to the airport. An amphitheater doubles as a flood catchment area, and the sinuous design mimics a natural river's ability to slow down flood waters. Seen from this little sliver of sylvan splendor, the towers of commerce seem to be from a different universe.

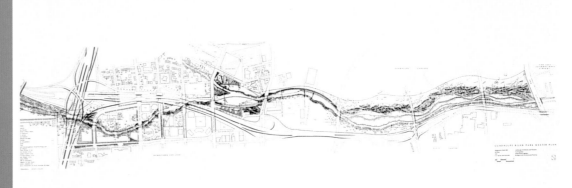

*above* amphitheater I *middle* site plan I *right and far right* pathways through park

*opposite* the urban context

# FOSTER AND PARTNERS
# GREAT GLASS HOUSE

The largest free-span dome in the world
(311 × 180 feet, 95 × 55 meters) is a low
oval stretched over and nestled into the
Welsh countryside, an abstract and smooth
shell rising up from its surroundings.
Visitors to the National Botanic Garden
of Wales enter down a ramp and through
a tunnel, emerging in a light-filled world
where the cliffs of the former quarry
have been transformed into areas
showing ecosystems from around the
globe. The abstraction of the architecture
is matched by landscape architect Kathryn
Gustafson's interpretations of natural
land forms.

*opposite, top* view from surrounding hills **|** *opposite,*
*bottom* cross section looking east **|** *above* exterior view
*left* plan **|** *below* roof detail

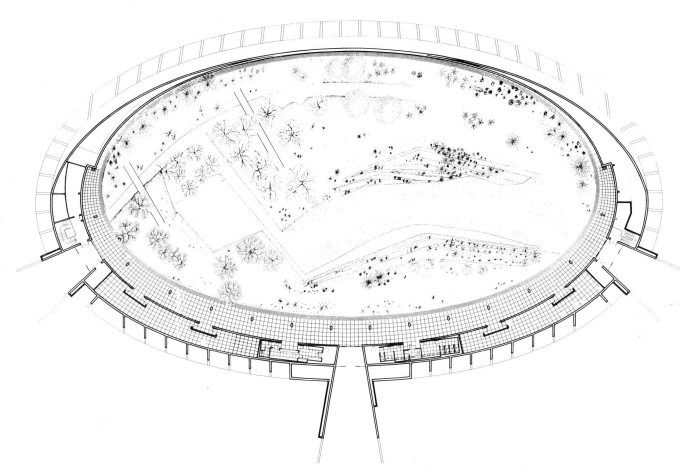

Shuhei Endo has hit on a simple idea: bending corrugated metal into curving ribbons that unfurl in parallel strips to create a rhythm of open and closed spaces. Endo's is a utopian vision for a whole city of open platforms through which these moments of shelter could be woven. He has constructed pieces of Springtecture for parks and small houses. Here, he proposes a fragment of his dream for an art museum complex at Aomori in the north-east of Japan.

*opposite and left* corrugated-metal shelters | *top left* site model | *above* distance view

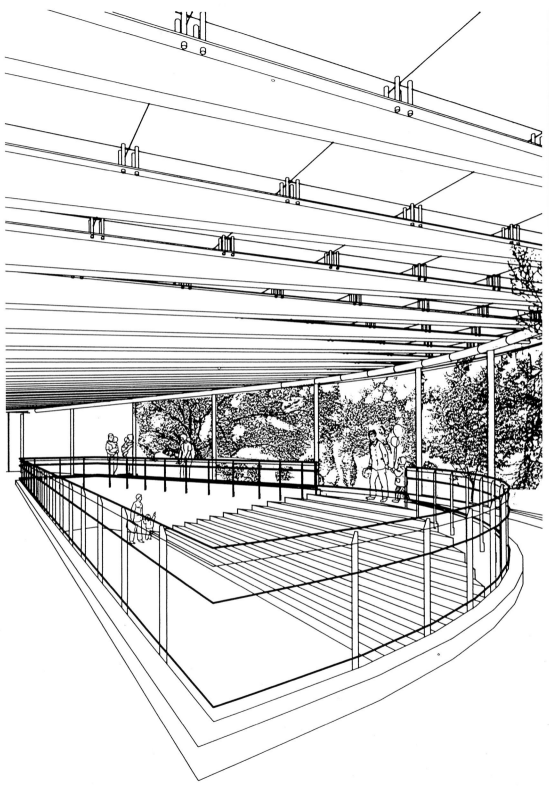

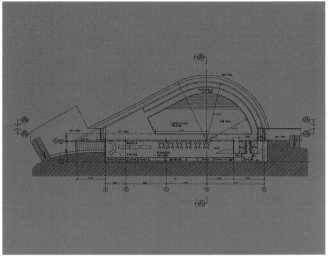

# IAN RITCHIE
# ARCHITECTS
## TERRASSON
## GREENHOUSE

From below, the greenhouse, in Terrasson-la-Villedieu, France, appears as an undulating retaining wall of loose rubble that protrudes out from a hillside landscape designed by Kathryn Gustafson. Citrus trees planted in front of the tall shape heighten the sense of a garden structure. From above, the impression is very different. Technology takes over in the form of a slightly angled roof that is bow-shaped in plan and made from glass.

*opposite, left* perspective drawing | *opposite, top right* cross section | *opposite, bottom right* retaining wall | *right* interior view | *far right* roof detail | *below* view from above

Stamping pure form into the earth was Dominique Perrault's response to the need for inserting an Olympic-scale velodrome in the middle of Berlin. Circular in shape, the velodrome rises no more than a meter above the ground and is surrounded by a grove of apple trees. Covered with shiny metal panels, it is a simple building dedicated to a single use and mass enjoyment. Perrault concentrated on the structure, especially the large, ring-shaped truss system over the velodrome, and the act of making a garden in which an abstract geometry marks man's common pursuit of perfection.

*opposite* **exterior view** I *left* **detail of metal panels** I *below* **interior view of roof**

# DOMINIQUE PERRAULT
## OLYMPIC VELODROME

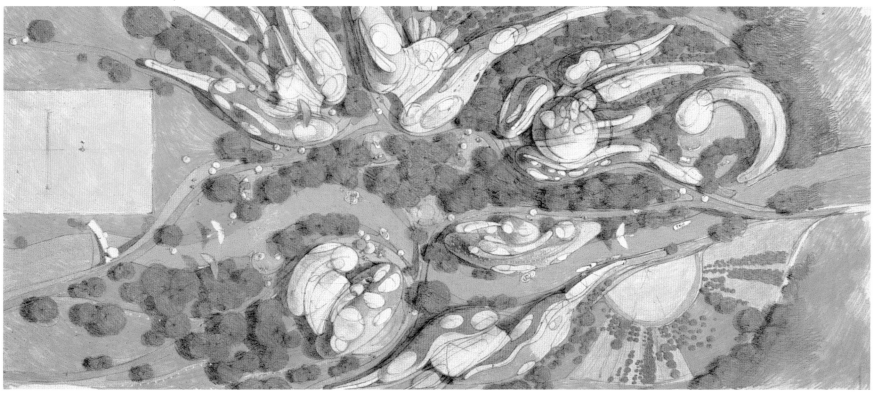

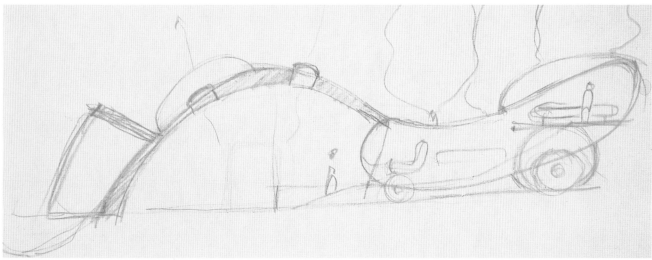

New York architect Michael Sorkin is known for his trenchant critiques of current architectural practice, and for the last few years he has been offering images of an alternative method of building. His evolving plans for an organic community dissolve the geometries used by previous generations of architects in favor of whirling, corkscrewing and undulating forms. House of the Future generates its own power and is constructed from biodegradable and recycled materials.

# MICHAEL SORKIN
# HOUSE OF THE FUTURE

*opposite* sketch of community | *above* aerial sketch

*left* sketch of house cross section

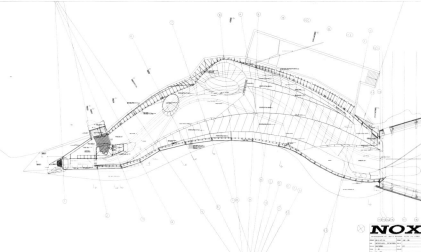

# NOX
# WATER
# PAVILION

In the Water Pavilion for the Delta Works, Neeltje Jans, the Netherlands, the edge between water and land becomes blurred. The fluidity of form expresses how the Dutch make land out of water and how water itself takes many forms to allow for transportation and field irrigation. The pavilion is a monument to an element that is threatening and life-giving. On the one hand, it is a timeless object whose abstraction yet brings to mind prehistoric creatures; on the other hand, it is a fluid sculpture of natural conditions, with shapes that are complex enough to demand continual interpretation or experience.

*top left and opposite* exterior views I *top right* plan I *right* interior view
*overleaf* entrance view

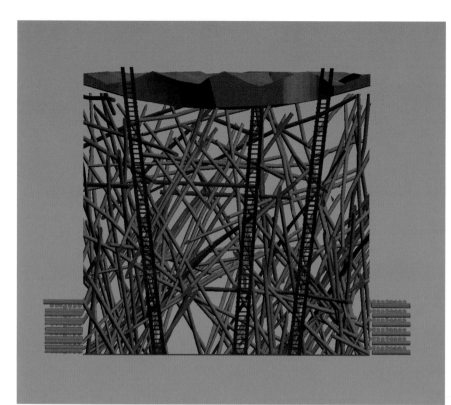

Playing God with nature at the Malmö Festival, Sweden, West 8 suggested a game of Mikado (pick-up sticks) using local logs. The logs had their ends painted red and were used to construct a perfect cube in the forest. They supported a roof in which several holes were cut to let light into the dense labyrinthine wood below. From the roof, a dense carpet of seashells spread out toward the nearby sea, developing a relationship between the sea and the Swedish forest.

*left* digital rendering | *below* exterior view | *below left* entrance pathway | *opposite, top* forest floor
*opposite, bottom* shell roof

# WEST 8
# SECRET GARDEN

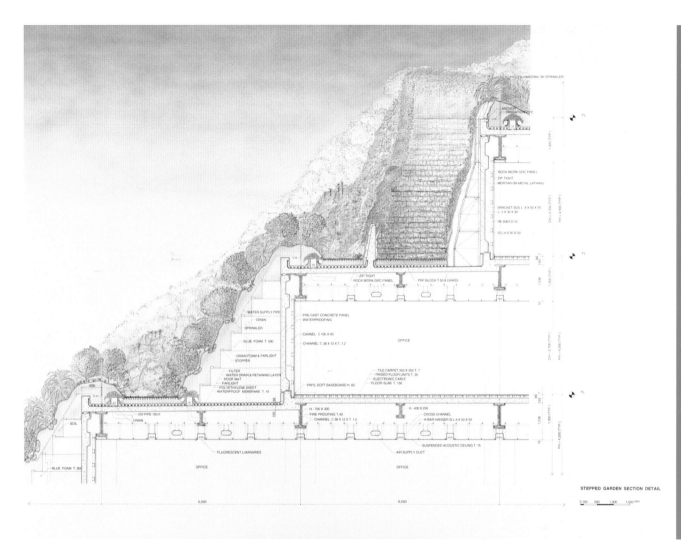

 One-million square feet (92,900 square meters) of office space and public halls is camouflaged by a terraced park in Fukuoka, Japan. From the street, the hall appears as a conventional, elegantly detailed office building; inside, fifteen levels of office space rise up around a central atrium.
It is only on the side facing the park that the building takes on another reality. A path zigzags up the terraces from the existing public park and users can ascend to the top of the building without feeling as if they have left public ground. From the top, they have a view of the city and of the green carpet that stretches out from the building's roof to cover the whole block.

STEPPED GARDEN SECTION DETAIL

*left* cross section | *below* view from park | *opposite, left* aerial view | *opposite, right* detail of terraced exterior

# EMILIO AMBASZ
# FUKUOKA PREFECTURAL INTERNATIONAL HALL

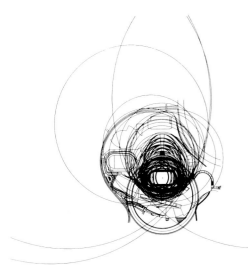

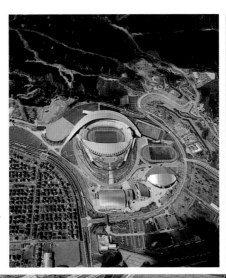

To construct a soccer stadium for fifty-thousand spectators in Sendai, Japan, Hitoshi Abe excavated part of a hill and then fitted two boomerang-shaped roofs over the bowl. These shapes provide shelter from the elements as well as the structure for the stadium's upper tiers. At either end of the pitch, the view to the surrounding park remains open so that visitors do not feel isolated in the vast new interior. The concrete substructure of sharply folded buttresses and columns makes visitors aware of the forces that allow these giant-scaled gestures to sail over a land that has been shaped from natural terrain into terraced park.

*above* sketch | *right and top right* aerial views

*opposite* ground-level view

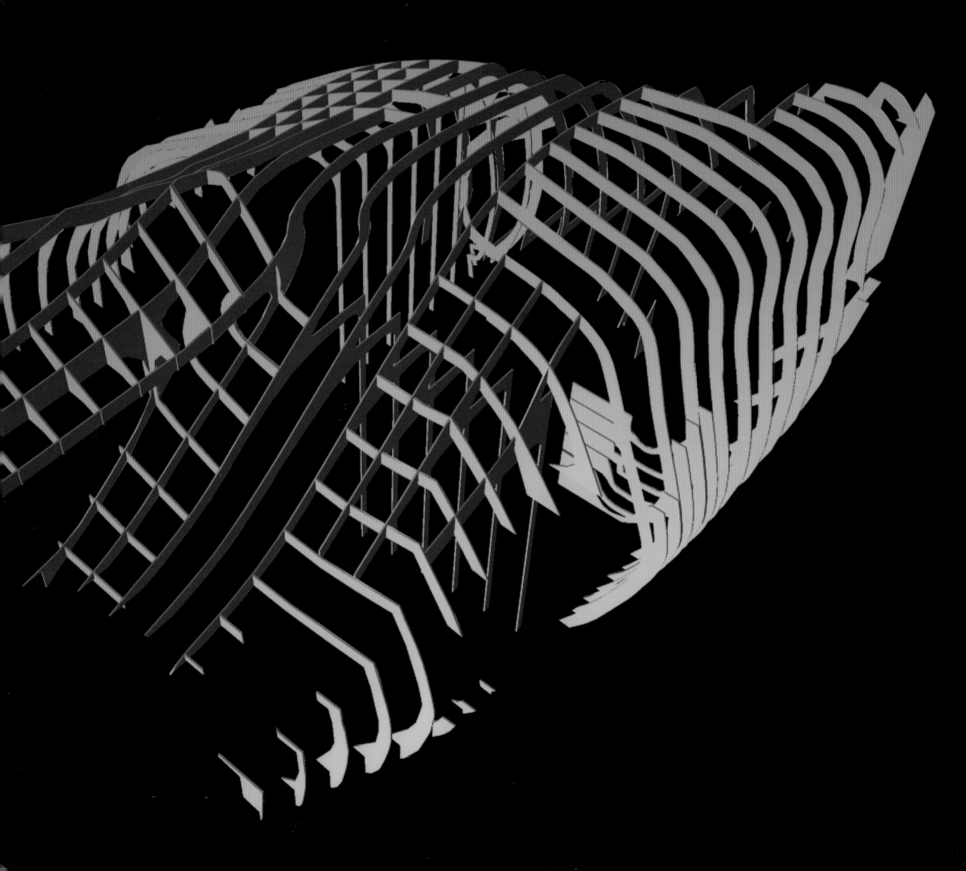

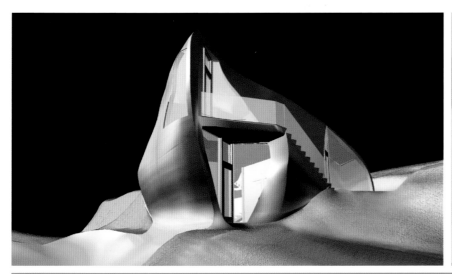

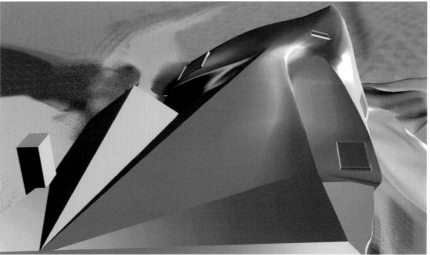

# KOLATAN/MAC DONALD STUDIO
# **RAYBOULD HOUSE**

In rural New England buildings stand on and out from the land. The white shapes of farm buildings and houses contrast with the rolling fields. New York architects Shulan Kolatan and Bill Mac Donald propose that the suburbanization of the area demands another kind of form: a house and garden in which the land and the protective shell for inhabitation have been merged through computer software. The result is a deformation of the existing building into an abstraction of the surrounding landscape.

*opposite* structural framework I *top left* exterior view I *top right and below* aerial views
*bottom left* entrance

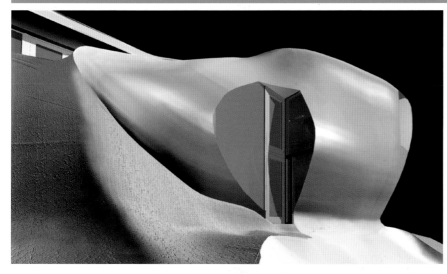

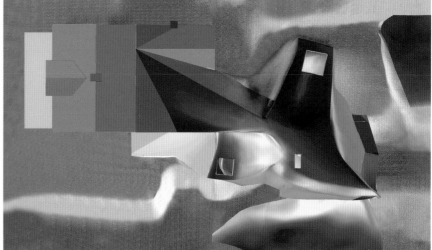

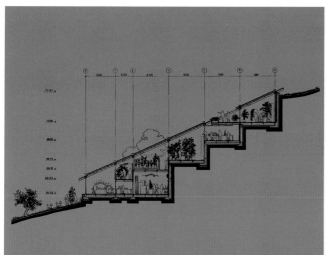

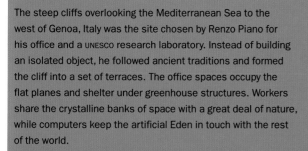

The steep cliffs overlooking the Mediterranean Sea to the west of Genoa, Italy was the site chosen by Renzo Piano for his office and a UNESCO research laboratory. Instead of building an isolated object, he followed ancient traditions and formed the cliff into a set of terraces. The office spaces occupy the flat planes and shelter under greenhouse structures. Workers share the crystalline banks of space with a great deal of nature, while computers keep the artificial Eden in touch with the rest of the world.

*opposite* aerial view of terraces | *clockwise, from top left* cross section; office space; interior view down the terraces; view of roof

# RENZO PIANO BUILDING WORKSHOP
## PUNTA NAVE BUILDING

# 2

## Caves and Caverns

Burrowing into the land to discover new spatial experiences

GIOVANNI BATTISTA PIRANESI **CARCERI**

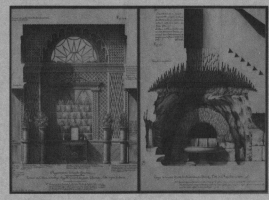

JEAN-JACQUES LEQUEU
**CHAMBER OF THE COUNCIL OF THE YOUNG GRACES** [LEFT]
**UNDERGROUND DESERT GROTTO** [RIGHT]

The alternative to building Towers of Babel has always been the retreat into caves. The earth is a place of return. To many, the cave we first found or made in the rocks is a reminder of the womb out of which we have come, and it may even be the first place in which human beings wove together a culture through a shared language and set of images. Certainly, caves are the earliest human habitations that still survive. To find the origins of who we are as human beings, we can descend into the depths of such caves as Lascaux to see the dreams of successful hunts and fertility displayed on walls.[1]

The cave is also the most basic underground structure. Although it has no particular form—it is merely a cavity hollowed out in the ground—it does have certain properties: a restricted opening, a sequence of spaces, an undefinable or unstable relationship between ground, walls and ceiling, and, of course, an essential darkness that human beings alone have been able to allay through the use of artificial light. Finally, it is a space of danger, because these very properties make it difficult to negotiate or understand, and its existence as a void always seems tenuous.

For many writers, the cave has only been the backdrop to an entire world that exists as an imaginary version of the one above,[2] for instance, Dante's *Inferno* and Jules Verne's *Journey to the Centre of the Earth*.[3] Only architects, it seems, have taken the cave seriously, trying to establish and elaborate its basic characteristics. Our interiors, however, are in many ways re-creations of such caves; they are not just what is enclosed by architecture, but places where we can dream of other worlds. Like the cave, the interior is in its essence a place of darkness and retreat. It is where we go, as bears do, to sleep, but also where we, like the early inhabitants of Lascaux, define a shared culture with paintings, mirrors, photographs of our loved ones, and furnishings that not only make us comfortable

but also bring faraway places and times into our small space. Chairs from seventeenth-century England, rugs from India and lamps from anonymous factories all create an environment that is a miniature version of our culture, arranged in a way that makes sense to us. This interior lies at the heart of our domestic structures.[4]

On a larger scale, we retire into dark caves to fantasize collectively: in theaters where actors stage alternate versions of reality, or where the screen flickers with an impossible world built from rays of light, jump cuts and zooms. We attend dark churches or temples to affirm our shared faith in something so far beyond understanding that we cannot articulate it. In these ways we erect *faux* caves that remove us from the rational structures of our everyday lives—edges blur, perspective disappears, we find ourselves staring at ourselves and the world we have made.

Both constructed interiors and caves have acted as generators for architectural movements. There was a great vogue for artificial caves in eighteenth-century France, and the forms architects and designers developed for these follies were so influential that they gave their name to the Rococo movement. Dripping with carved stone, the caves were meant to refine the natural shapes of stalagmites for the enjoyment of the upper classes. Furthermore, they evoked the archae-ological digs that at the time were producing a wealth of classical artifacts on which scholars and artists sought to base a revived and revised society. The caves also had a feeling of the hidden, the dangerous, the illicit that legitimized the hidden pleasures of the upper classes. Caves reconnected their occupants to something that had been lost: a civilization, nature, or their own bodies.[5]

A different take on the cave was the starting point for the architecture of Giovanni Battista Piranesi (1720–78) and Jean-

Jacques Lequeu (1757–1825). At the beginning of the West's fascination with its ability to make spaces whose scale and location defied standard methods of judgment or viewing, architects realized that caves could form counter-cultures. Piranesi's work has often been linked to the achievements of painters and writers, such as Francisco Goya (1746–1828) who found within the rationalization of the world the potential for its own self-destruction in *The Sleep of Reason Produces Monsters* (1797–98). There is a relationship of equal importance, however, between Piranesi's famous *Carceri* (1744–47) and the mines and dungeons that helped to produce the wealth for the Enlightenment, to say nothing of the catacombs present throughout the Rome where Piranesi worked.[6] Perhaps his visions of a frighteningly incompre-hensible underground world were not aberrations of rationality so much as the turning of the underground world that had always existed into the kind of architecture that might rival the Baroque churches then rising above ground.

In a similar vein, the work of the supremely perverse Lequeu tried to develop the world of the repressed and suppressed femininity that painters, such as French Rococo artist Jean-Antoine Watteau (1684–1721), had graced with their brush. The voluptuous chambers Lequeu drew took the enclosed bed, the layers of clothes and the boudoir and transformed this hidden system of sexuality into the neo-classical language men were trying to impose on the central institutions of the French state.[7]

In the twentieth and twenty-first centuries, such impulses have gained new urgency. The fear of mass destruction has led countries to build vast underground shelters and to anticipate that we might at some point in the future have to abandon all structures on the face of the earth. Yet, the desire to build modern caves comes not just from fear. It is also the result of

LE CORBUSIER **MAISONS JAOUL**

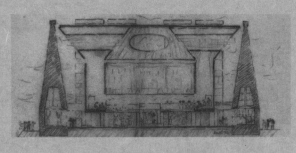

LOUIS I. KAHN **HURVA SYNAGOGUE (SECTION OF THIRD SCHEME)**

ALVAR AALTO **SÄYNÄTSALO TOWN HALL**

architects' conscious attempt to go back to some form of—perhaps imagined—original state, and to make buildings that do not take open space away from communal enjoyment or use. At their best, the new caves express the tension between fear and generosity, between retreat and exploration of new terrain, and between closed form and open plane. Just as the flat heroic held these tensions in its forms, so the new caves are open to contrasting possibilities.[8]

The rediscovery of the cave started in the 1930s at the same time as our culture was beginning to mine and picture the subconscious. Paintings that delved into the deepest recesses of the land produced imagery whose fluidity presaged the flat heroic. Furthermore, surrealist art proposed the need for organic shapes that would return us to an awareness of our body and its secrets. Doubts about the efficacy or desirability of the vast structures of rationality that were being self-consciously decreed for the earth fed the retreat into the cave.[9]

The architect who gave clearest form to these desires was Le Corbusier. His Maisons Jaoul in Neuilly-sur-Seine (1952–56) were the result of explorations into surreal space, as was his own apartment interior and the Bestigui Apartment. In Maisons Jaoul, Le Corbusier reintroduced a sense of materiality, weight and gravity that he had excised from his earlier buildings. He reached back to ancient traditions, drawing on such structures as catacombs, aqueducts, storage areas and caves to create concrete embodiments of the force of nature.[10]

The most luminous of these buildings is the pilgrimage chapel of Notre Dame-du-Haut in Ronchamp (1950–55). While the building has been compared to everything from a tent to a nun's wimple, the reality is a heavy roof that floats over planes that continually recede before the eye. There is no façade, only a lifting or stretching up of the ground. Inside, a luminous

space opens up: the ground slopes down and in, the walls slope out, and it feels as if we have entered another realm. The cave is a transformative space where we can reject the worries of the modern world and focus on a direct contemplation of ourselves and our place in relation to something immense and abstract.

Cavernous spirituality also comes through in certain projects designed by American architect Louis I. Kahn (1901–74). His buildings have a ruinous quality, as if they were fragments from a primitive past we have only now rediscovered, or as if acknowledging the dissolution of our confident civic structures in the period of self-doubt that set in during the 1960s. They turn inward. Kahn's project for the Hurva Synagogue in Jerusalem (1967–74) is a good example. It is based on a conjectural excavation of the Temple of Solomon, and is a space that has been dug out, leaving supports to shore up the earth around it. These buttresses are occupiable nooks, with light washing down their sloped façades into the rest of the building. The main sanctuary floats within this light and is carved out between its own massive piers and surmounted by a flared roof. The plan is in fact based on a grid of isolated cells that somehow come together to make a set of experiences. Kahn sought to carve out a world of shade and shadows within the synagogue. He perceived such spaces as sanctuaries where we could go back to discover the essence of our communal institutions, places where we could gather to explore, discuss and ritually fix a common purpose.[11]

Kahn's closed and introverted bastions and spirituality continue to feature in our designs of religious structures and museums, but his searching solemnity has proven to be too dark for most other uses. Similarly, Alvar Aalto spent four decades designing inward-turned libraries, performance

spaces and city halls that externally appeared as natural components of the landscape while sheltering internal spaces for communal gathering. Aalto made humble structures that twisted up from the ground plane as if a great force had pushed up the earth and opened up a space inside it. This type of interior always spreads and moves us toward light, for example, through the splayed and skylit nooks of the Seinäjoki City Library (1960–65), or through the gentle wash of light in the Säynätsalo Town Hall (1949, 1950–52), both in Aalto's native Finland. The forms are lighter and smaller than those Kahn decreed, but they also mitigate against reproduction by other architects.[12]

The last heroic masters of modernism—Le Corbusier, Kahn and Aalto—carved out these places of retreat to return us to the basics of building as a communal act of faith in constructing a new world. Other architects, however, began to make caves as a rational response to existing conditions. Hans Hollein's brief for the Abteiberg Museum in Mönchengladbach, Germany (1972–82), for instance, was to make a cultural institution that would not displace a municipal park and would not be an alien entity proposing high culture to the city's inhabitants. His solution is a building that appears to be underground, although he actually re-created the existing conditions of the sloped land. The galleries are labyrinths without clear direction, so that the visitor can become lost in this cave of culture. Fragmented and formless, the museum shows the importance of culture not as a fact, but as a possibility to be pieced together by the individual.[13]

During the 1970s, British architect James Stirling (1926–92) suggested several new caves for cultural institutions. The most radical of these, the Wallraf-Richartz Museum (1975) next to the cathedral in Cologne, was never

constructed. Stirling wanted to carve out the cathedral's plan to make a central courtyard within an artificial plinth, whose volume would contain the museum. The spaces within the block would be dissected by paths. In the case of the extensions to the Staatsgalerie in Stuttgart (1977–84), the building resembles a cliff, with its undulating wall sitting atop ramps and with views over the downtown area. Inside, galleries are based around a grid, the edges of which give way to a flowing wall overlooking the city. At the heart of the complex is a circular space. Open to the sky, it is not so much a moment within the museum as a pause along a public path that leads from the residential neighborhood above to the city below. Here, the cave has become an outdoor space sheltered by the museum. It allows visitors to feel as if they are part of, or at least surrounded by, culture without being buried within it. Instead of the drive to a burial and then a rebirth into something spiritual or artful, Stirling proposes a period of immersion that is tentative and open-ended.[14]

This ambivalence about the nature of caves has its purest expression in Maya Lin's 1982 Vietnam Veterans Memorial in Washington, D.C. (see p. 72). The monument starts as a simple line in the grass that grows into a plane as one sinks below the horizon. First one name appears, then several, until the visitor is overcome by the names of all those who died in Vietnam. As the list grows, visitors move ever further below the earth, losing all sense of the open space they have just left behind. The walls rise up, cutting off views and overwhelming the narrow slot of space. Standing at the bottom of the memorial, the names stretch out to either side and visitors feel isolated from the confident white forms that surround the greensward. The sky is still there, though, and so is a sense of hope or escape. The dark incision into the ground opens up to resemble a crypt, but never distances the visitor from the fields of democracy on which that same war was the subject of so many protests.[15]

Lin explores the idea of memorial in simple forms in several other projects, but nowhere has the engagement with the land reached such a level of intensity as in the Vietnam memorial. It seems that the simple act of 'almost burial' gives focus to any activity that takes place below ground. Such is certainly the case in the thermal baths designed by Peter Zumthor for the small town of Vals in the Swiss Alps (1990–96, see p. 78). The baths are reached by a winding, narrow road that leads to the end of a valley. Visitors then move up through the hotel, and then back down into a set of black-painted corridors. There, they enter a realm of water-filled rooms that respond to the ritual of bathing with a rhythm of rectilinear walls and columns of green granite. The cave has become an abstracted ruin with views to the surrounding Alps.

In 1996, Enric Miralles (1955–2000) and Carme Pinós completed Igualada cemetery in Barcelona (see p. 76). The monumental axes proper to such places of reverence for the dead are transformed into fragmentary incisions into the landscape that lead to cave-like harbors within the rocks where the urns are kept. The architects did not so much abandon the traditional form of the cemetery as they created a more unstable relationship between its placid fields of remembrance and what the planes cover.

While Miralles and Pinós work with such fundamental issues as death and violence (ritualized in burial), William Bruder designed his Deer Valley Rock Art Center, Arizona (1996, see p. 86) to weave together the ancient and the new. The center guides visitors to the site of Native American petroglyphs that survive on desert boulders, and is part of a dam, holding back the extremely occasional floods that wash down the desert and threaten the surrounding suburban community. On arrival at the center, visitors are funneled into a narrow space that curves past exhibits and then opens up again to the landscape. The building proper consists of tilt-up concrete panels covered with slag, the tailings of copper mines: the violence man has committed to the landscape is turned into a beautiful fabric. The dark interior traces the line of the dam and offers a structured and logical commentary on the landscape and the petroglyphs before releasing visitors from the cavern to confront the sheer power of the ancient and new forms. Bruder's simple design opens us up to a much wider realization of the tangled web humans have woven for over three millennia between the land and themselves.

Japanese architect Norihiko Dan registered his interest in earthworks in his bath house in the Tosa Shimizu Citizens' Hostel (1996–98). The baths are situated in the side of a hill, in small cubes that look out over the sea and that are separated from each other by concrete walls. The entire structure seems to regularize the hill into a grid of cleanliness and clarity.

Rick Joy adapts rammed-earth forms to the exigencies of modern living in his houses in Arizona. Their heavy forms and small windows protect inhabitants from the desert sun, turning the interiors into cool oases. Joy is interested in the sculptural presence of his forms, manipulating them to compose layered vistas and highly regularized shapes. Drawing on the vernacular of pueblo architecture and the simple courtyard houses built by Spanish settlers in the area, he finds a modernist desire to weed out ornamentation and excess construction to reveal the most basic ways one can inhabit the earth.

Certainly, the cave as place of sensual retreat has a long history. Furthermore, aside from being associated with origins (the womb) and ends (burial), the cave has another use: the

SVERRE FEHN **HEDMARK CATHEDRAL MUSEUM**

SVERRE FEHN **GLACIER MUSEUM**

location where we come to terms with ourselves, our body and our society.[16] Perhaps this is what Rem Koolhaas had in mind when he wrote his seminal critique of New York, *Delirious New York*, in 1978.[17] He describes skyscrapers as the super-ego of the city's hidden ego, which is found in the pleasure palaces the city has hollowed out in the innermost part of these soaring structures. The individuality of the palaces is protected by the repetitive grid of the skyscraper and justifies the expense of the giant structures above them. Pleasure palaces used the latest technology to create a fantasy world inside the skyscraper, a world celebrated by such novelists as F. Scott Fitzgerald (1896–1940), and one that still survives to this day.[18] Its ultimate symbol is the globe at the heart of Raymond Hood's Daily News Building (c. 1930)—all the world could be contained inside the skyscraper's massive blocks.

Most structures of internal delight merely continued and intensified the already dense urban life outside. New York's Peacock Alley, cutting through the behemoth that is the Waldorf-Astoria Hotel (1931), turned into the underground labyrinth that stretches out below the Rockefeller Center. Removed from the confines of the city grid above and outside, these spaces of sensual enjoyment reach out into the bowels of the earth, tying themselves around the circulation systems of subways, walkways and escalators that animate the city. These Aladdin's caves of commercial wealth have now popped up all over the world, becoming especially popular underneath the train stations of Asia. As they grow larger and more mundane, they lose the excitement their constricted forebears presented to the metropolitan wanderer. It was the guilty pleasure of commerce and places of play combined with the labyrinthine quality of the space that made the Rockefeller Center such a miraculous cave.

Today, such delights continue in the discos and rave parties that hollow out a technological spectacle for dancers inside warehouses all over the world. These are the contemporary caves where one goes to retreat from the conventions of the outside world. Here, it is always night, the body is central, time and space are dissolved by the artificial rhythm that transforms the dancer into a piece of a communal artifact. In contrast to the purely spiritual realm of the church or temple, the isolation of the rave party from the outside world does not so much liberate the mind as it frees the body. As a direct outgrowth of the baths and other venues of pleasure seeking that have traditionally hidden underground, the dance cave is our current celebration of the unconstrained. As something that is tied directly to the air conditioning, electricity wires and other ganglia snaking through and underneath our buildings, the techno-cave rejoices in the hidden innards of the city's body while making us exercise our own.

Few architects touch these caves, which seem to express our desire to get away from everything we associate with architecture. They are not places of rational, functional and clean lines. They do not make sense. They do not explain how they work, they do not limit our movement, and they do not frame our experience. Instead, all form disintegrates. The body itself stands out, a body that is now completely animated and reflected by technology. Whether it is in the light and sound shows of the disco or the mirrored window fronts of the underground shopping arcade, these new caves give us back to ourselves as we dissolve into the world we have made for ourselves, a world that is threatening to turn us into mere fragments caught in a sprawling mechanism. The cave is as close as we come to experiencing the effect of the technology that is creating the global spread of a networked and digitized economy.

This is not to say that we do not hark back to the original use of the cave, and architects continue to argue that the cave is a place we can learn from. Massimiliano Fuksas's entrance pavilion to the prehistoric cave paintings of Niaux in France convey this use of the cave (see p. 90). Completed in 1995, his platform of steel plates slices out from the mouth of the cave. As one moves into the maws of the sharply angled planes, the outside world is dissected into thin slivers of view. The angles also give the illusion that the space is shorter and the skies are even more distant. A winding path leads the visitor into the caves themselves, where architecture stops.

Norwegian architect Sverre Fehn investigates the potential of caves in several projects. In Hedmark Cathedral Museum (Norway, 1967–79) visitors move through concrete forms placed into and atop stone walls to find themselves lost in a labyrinth, which covers an open space where the excavations can be explored. Visitors walk on and below a new fabric whilst surrounded by the old ruins. Tension between old and new turns into a route of discovery in which the two states are not presented as opposites but as relatives.

The Glacier Museum in Fjaerland (Norway, 1989–91) is an artificial cave. Visitors use the building as a plinth by walking on the roof to view the glacier. On entering the building, the space does not open up into a new realm; instead, visitors circulate around the edges of a long and narrow room, the center of which is occupied by exhibits. Light filters down through clerestory windows. The museum acts as a bunker protecting the visitor from the glaciers, while re-creating the feeling of being caught in a glacial crevasse.

Steven Holl's addition to the Nelson-Atkins Museum of Art in Kansas City, Missouri (1999–present, see p. 92), is a much gentler affair. Burrowing underground, he creates a sequence of galleries below the symmetrical and classical world of the

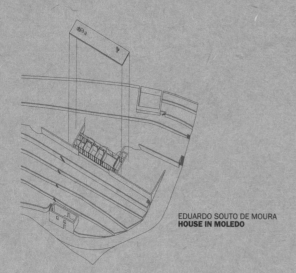

EDUARDO SOUTO DE MOURA
**HOUSE IN MOLEDO**

UN STUDIO **VILLA WILBRINK**

original building and its gardens. The only mark the project leaves on ground level is a set of vaguely v-shaped skylights that allow light to filter down onto the plaster walls inside. Underground, Holl has organized seven interconnected galleries around T-shaped walls that allow light and air to circulate freely around their tops. As structural and lighting elements, the walls bring to mind those of Kahn's synagogue, although Holl's are on a much smaller scale and without the monumental clarity of the temple. As caves, the galleries are not so much places of retreat as tents that replace the outside world with a gentle and more focused version of itself.

An even simpler cave is the Multimedia Workshop designed by Kazuyo Sejima + Ryue Nishizawa/SANAA in Ooqaki, Japan (1996–97, see p. 84). Amid the confusion of the suburban landscape, the architects created a green field out of which a mesh tower rises. The tower hints at the simplicity of the box that lurks under a slightly bowed, grass-covered roof. Entering along a long ramp, visitors find themselves sinking below the level of the familiar and into a new and luminous world dedicated to exploring the creative possibilities of new technologies.

Portuguese architect Eduardo Souto de Moura designed a similar structure. The House in Moledo (1991–97) is a glass box that stands in a cliff, covered by a single roof plane. Souto de Moura camouflaged its form in terraces that present a regularized version of the stone hillside. A glass façade opens up to the view below. At the back of the house, a continuous band of glass faces the sculpture of rocks that he excavated to make room for the house.

Dutch firm Neutelings Riedijk has gone even further to re-create the sensation of being underground in their Minnaert Building at the University of Utrecht (1994–98, see p. 70), situated in the middle of a former meadow. Because it is home

to the university's earth-sciences department, the architects clad the building in spray-on concrete that they furrowed to resemble abstract ridges. The façade's composition does not follow the rules of good taste and is not meant to be judged as a freestanding block. Rather, it is intended as a man-made mesa marooned on the campus. Entering, one climbs large steps to a cave at the building's heart. Water gathered from the roof trickles in through fountains in the walls and collects in a shallow pool into which the floor slopes down. Students can sit in red booths along one wall as if in small recesses. An adjacent computer room appears to be another cave, with the only natural light coming from a skylight far above walls painted like a starry sky.

Can anyone actually imagine inhabiting such caves? Some architects think that we can and should. While nobody is proposing that we move back into the mountains, certain architects are creating artificial caves by lifting up more modest and mundane subterranean places. A good example is UN Studio's Villa Wilbrink in Amersfoort, the Netherlands (1992–94, see p. 88). The house starts as a gravel plane that slopes up to become the roof. The architect describes the house as a bunker, and it certainly gives the impression of a defensive structure. Here, "home, sweet home" is only made possible by a radical removal of the outside world. Inside, the spaces are simple and inward turned. The only views out are toward a contained and controlled garden with a minimum of plant life. The walls and ceiling crease and fold to define the contours within which domestic functions take place. There are few stable reference points, only the continual slope toward a space of retreat.

Toyo Ito's house for his sister (1985) was an even more extreme retreat from the encircling city. Presenting nothing but a concrete wall to Tokyo, it was a tube of space, like a section

of a subway, surrounded by a tiny courtyard. It was a self-contained and continuous fragment of domestic space. Shifting levels mimicked tectonic plates, but the tube always suggested a certain logic that was yet without sense because it had no articulation. Sadly, the house was torn down in 1999 to make way for a larger, more rational and "above-ground" development.

The Guest House James Cutler built in 1996 in computer billionaire Bill Gates's compound in Seattle, Washington, however, is a much more reassuring affair. As in the Villa Wilbrink, guests enter the space by sliding in-between walls around which the ground rises. Once inside, the space opens up to a view of the forest, and the bedrooms and living room find definition in walls Cutler has articulated with great care. All the details, down to the hand-forged iron connections lashing together the major structural beams, seem well-crafted and make guests aware of the house's construction. Yet it is not possible to lose the feeling of being in a cave. A concrete wall appears to erode to reveal a stone fireplace whose neo-primitive design is highlighted by a skylight that washes its face with sunlight. Smooth wood surfaces rise out of what look like excavations in the ground and up into what looks like a ruin the architect found on the site. The cave is a fragment of a new order emerging out of a new-found ground.

In other words, the cave grounds and houses us—as long as we have a way out. Architects seem unwilling to take us all the way back into its recesses. We need light, air, and a connection to the outside world of reason and construction to prevent the cave from taking us back into ourselves, our past and our mind. Architects do not want to isolate us unless they can excuse their acts by designing buildings that demand spiritual commitment. Only non-architects allow us a hedonistic enjoyment without reference to the outside world.

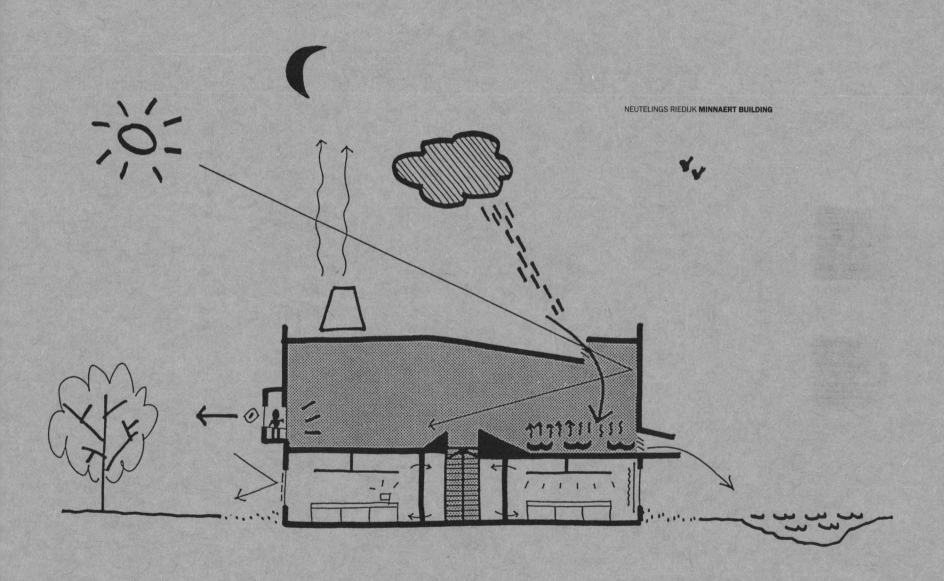

One exception is visionary architect Lebbeus Woods, although his structures are unbuilt and quite probably unbuildable. In 1988, the wizard of pencil renderings imagined a world that existed somewhere below one of the world's strangest and most tense capital cities. *Underground Berlin* sketched a society using the subway and sewage channels that had once tied the German capital together, but had then been severed by the Berlin Wall. Woods created a group of outlaws that made the labyrinth their own, and began to enlarge it into chambers lined with steel plates and shot through with electrical wires. A new kind of architecture appeared whose forms merged images of an armor-plated version of the body with what looked like the tectonic plates out of which our earth is composed. By a bulging out of space and through cracks and fissures, places were made. The inhabitants filled the spaces with equipment. The function of this underground society, Woods speculated, was nothing more than to calibrate the energies of the earth to those of the human body. As a result, a community could replace the artificial bonds of society with ones that were more organic, basic and fundamental. By going back into the roots of the city and boring through the soil out of which we came, Woods hoped to find an architecture and society that would save us from the vaunting ambitions we had erected above ground before they came crashing down under the weight of their internal contradictions.

At the end of the series of images, Woods showed the society erupting out of its caverns and taking aim at the city above. Cracking open a public square at the heart of the city, the architecture became a hybrid of a monster, a human figure and a building. It answered the rules of orthogonal propriety with a machine-like beauty emerging from the deep. Woods continued his myth in a second series, *Aerial Paris*

(1989), which depicted this same society dancing over the roofs of Paris before going on to Berlin and several other cities to bore out new spaces of liberation from abandoned apartment buildings that had been damaged by such armed conflicts as the Second World War and those in the former Yugoslavia.[19]

Woods does not suggest that the architecture he drew out of the caverns underneath Berlin is either real or liberating, yet he sketches it so that we can believe in it. He draws the possibility of something new from an imagined place below what we know. It is this idea of unfolding the earth and exposing what may lie underground that has generated some of the most explicit landscrapers of the last few years.

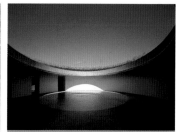

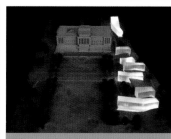

# FUMIHIKO MAKI
# KAZE-NO-OKA CREMATORIUM

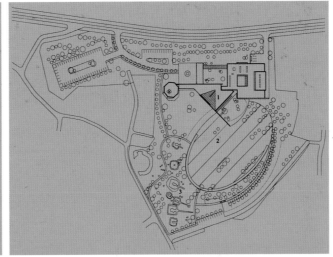

When the site was being prepared for a new crematorium in Nakatsu, Japan, ancient burial grounds were found, thus encouraging Fumihiko Maki to pursue a strategy in which the building was almost invisible from the outside. With long pathways, defined by horizontal and vertical planes that seem to hover above the earth, Maki draws the procession from arrival through the ceremony and the cremation and out into the open air. Interior volumes are more unstable and fragmentary, as if they are pieces of order the architect has hollowed out from the more permanent spaces of the earth.

*opposite* interior view I *left* chapel I *above* exterior view

*above left* site plan

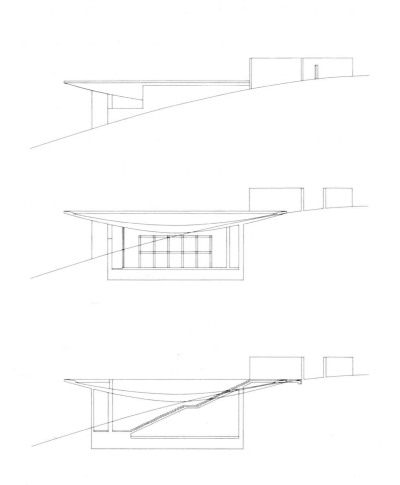

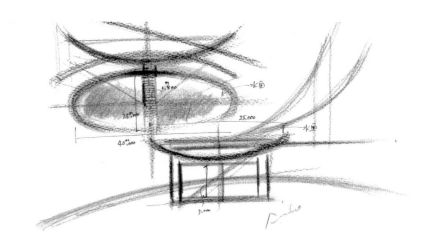

# TADAO ANDO
## HOMPUKUJI
## WATER TEMPLE

In one of this often bombastic minimalist's most convincing sleights of hand, a Buddhist temple disappears under an elliptical pool on Awaji Island, Japan. The below-ground sanctuary takes the same shape as the lily pond above. Visitors descend into the complex by a narrow set of stairs that slices through the almost-too-perfect surface. The insistent geometry of the temple appears as a series of thin lines in the landscape and as light-filled caverns below the surface.

*opposite, left* side elevation and cross sections | *opposite, top* sketch | *opposite, bottom* aerial view of pool | *below and right* interior views of temple

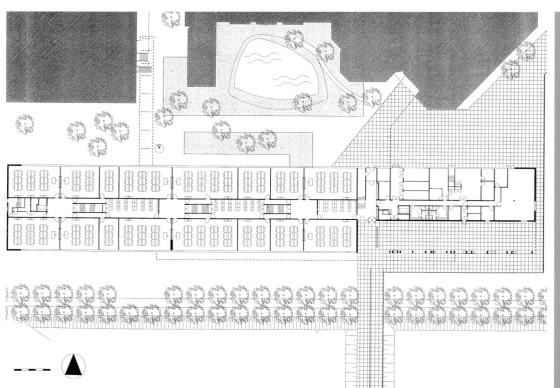

The architects covered a building, which serves as a student and facilities center for the study of the earth, with their own version of the land: red-pigmented spray-on concrete. The building at the University of Utrecht refuses to hide in the ground or stand against it, but seems to dress up in the earth in acceptance of its function. Inside, the major space is a dark cavern where rainwater, collected on the roof, seeps into a sloping pool that extends from the walkways.

*opposite, top* lobby | *opposite, bottom left* study booths | *opposite, bottom right* lecture hall | *left* ground-level plan | *below* exterior view

# NEUTELINGS RIEDIJK
## MINNAERT BUILDING

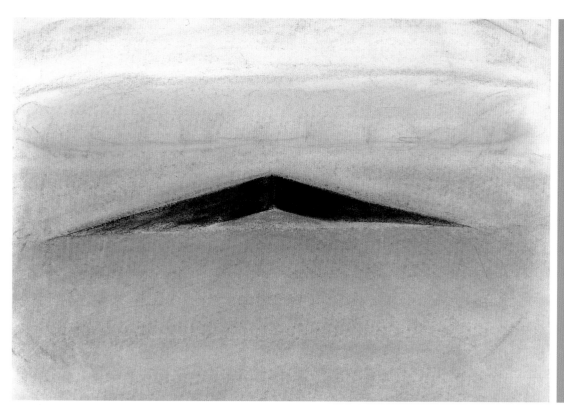

The v-shaped memorial in Washington, D.C. starts and ends as a single line of stone in the ground. As visitors walk down a sloping path, the line becomes a wall and rises up until it towers above them. At the same time, the one name visitors see incised in the black granite at the path's origin becomes a sea of names in which individual identity is lost. This potent evocation of the dark and senseless nature of war stands against the white memorials plunked down on the rest of Washington's monumental Mall.

*left* architect's painting | *below* aerial view | *opposite, top left* memorial's sloping path
*opposite, right and bottom left* wall of names

# MAYA LIN
# VIETNAM VETERANS MEMORIAL

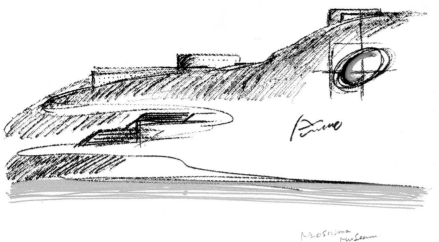

# TADAO ANDO
# NAOSHIMA CONTEMPORARY ART MUSEUM

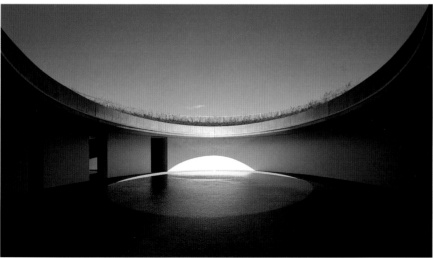

Arriving on the small island of Naoshima, Japan, visitors to the art museum walk up a stepped plaza that also serves as an outdoor amphitheater and houses museum offices. The main gallery is a completely underground skylit space, located in a half-submerged structure on the hill. In 1995, Ando added a second gallery further uphill, which opens up to an ovoid pool sunk in the earth. Too sophisticated and precise to be an earthwork, the museum is a highly refined insertion of man-made space in a landscape that the architect perceives as dominant, but answers with his own assertions of concrete order.

*opposite* interior exhibition space | *top left* sketch | *top right* aerial view | *above and left* oval pool

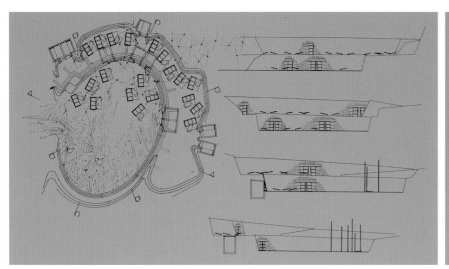

# ENRIC MIRALLES AND CARME PINÓS
## IGUALADA CEMETERY

Faced with the task of turning an existing stone quarry in an industrial area of Igualada, Spain into a cemetery, Miralles and Pinós devised a site strategy that draws visitors away from their surroundings and into the envelopment of the hills. The burial niches become regularizations and articulations of the hillside, and the chapel is completely underground. Only a few pieces of wall remain to help direct views and to serve the cemetery, leaving the impression that you are surrounded by the ruins of an urban setting excavated and reinhabited by an architect turned archaeologist.

*top left* ground-level plan and sections of burial niches
*left* walls of burial niches I *opposite, top left* detail of interlocking concrete panels I *opposite, bottom left* interior view I *opposite, right* toplit circulation space

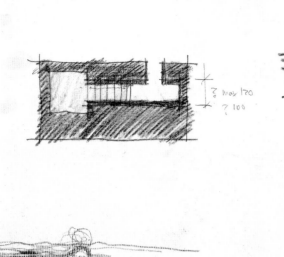

At the end of a long and winding road into the Swiss Alps is a hotel and thermal baths. In the basement, guests enter a dark environment where narrow bands of green granite stack up to enclose a tight rhythm of chambers. On leaving the changing rooms, a cavelike expanse of water opens up, where light filters down over the stone to illuminate the pools of warm, tepid and cold water. Separate, dark chambers provide complete isolation in which aromas or sounds take over from sight. After immersion in this other world, guests swim under a glass plate to see the Alpine Valley stretching out around an outdoor swimming pool. The journey has brought guests back into reality, cleansed and with heightened senses.

*opposite* exterior view | *left* sketch | *bottom left* plan | *below and p. 81* green granite interiors | *overleaf* view of pool

# PETER ZUMTHOR
# THERMAL BATHS

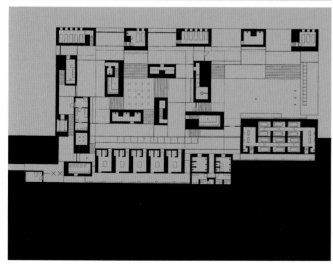

# FRANÇOIS ET ASSOCIÉS
# LARRENGUADE TUNNEL

This competition-winning project in France proposes a scenographic re-staging of nature. Instead of expressing technology, it seeks to restore nature. The tunnel entrance is designed to look like a picture-postcard view of a nearby cave where archaeological remains have been found. A fissure heightens the idea of a natural topography restored. Near the actual construction, ancient forests and many native plants were to have been introduced to form a dense carpet of vegetation around the motorway.

*this page* the tunnel was designed to remind visitors of the rich prehistoric remains in the region | *opposite* plants were chosen for their red coloring throughout the seasons

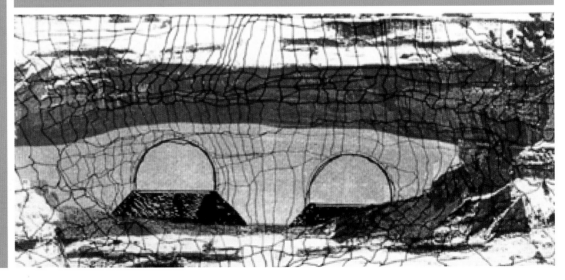

# KAZUYO SEJIMA + RYUE NISHIZAWA/SANAA
## MULTIMEDIA WORKSHOP

A suburban cave, the Multimedia Workshop is located in the middle of a green expanse on the International Academy of Media Arts and Sciences campus in Gifu, Japan. The building can be accessed via the bowed, grass-covered roof, which is also used by students for outdoor exhibitions. A long ramp leads the visitor down into this creative cavern, which is sunk nearly six feet into the ground.

*top* campus setting | *middle and opposite* entrance ramp
*left and far left* interior circulation spaces

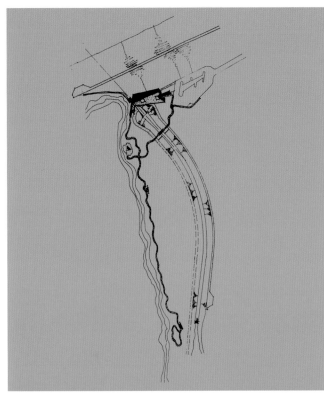

# WILLIAM BRUDER
# DEER VALLEY ROCK ART CENTER

Using the structure of a small dam to protect a new suburban community in Phoenix, Bruder has also created a visitor center and a path that heads toward an outcrop showing Native American petroglyphs. The curving road along the dam leads the visitor to a set of angled walls covered in concrete panels encrusted with shale, the waste product of the area's mining tradition. The building is a reminder of man's interference in nature, making us aware of how we mark the land.

*clockwise, from top left* site plan; interior views of visitor center | *opposite, top* view from nearby hillside | *opposite, bottom left* entrance | *opposite, bottom right* plan

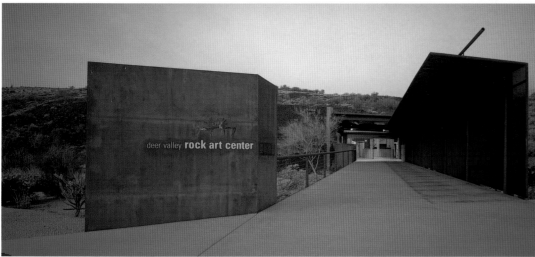

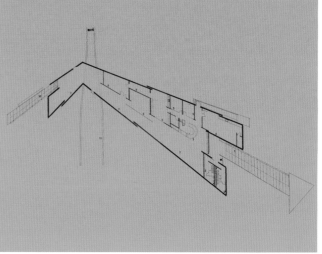

In the middle of a suburban neighborhood in Amersfoort, the Netherlands, a plane of pebbles slants upward. Incredibly, it is the home of a family who wanted to close themselves off from their surroundings and did not want to maintain a garden. With this in mind, architects at UN Studio drew inspiration from bunkers. Visitors enter the house down a narrow path between the roof plane, and find themselves immediately in the middle of the living areas, which group around a small patio. The materials are simple, even harsh, emphasizing the notion that this is a defensive habitation.

*opposite* patio | *right* back façade | *below* view from street

# UN STUDIO
# **VILLA WILBRINK**

# MASSIMILIANO FUKSAS
## ENTRANCE PAVILION

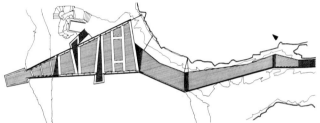

The entrance pavilion to the prehistoric cave paintings of Niaux in France extends the original cave into the surrounding landscape. The structure of steel plates slices open the cave's mouth along a platform that is built into the cliffs, forming a man-made equivalent to the enclosure where one sees the paintings. The visitor enters between the plates and is led from the complexities of the outside world into an ever darker and more concentrated space, until the architecture stops and the caves take over.

*opposite* the entrance pavilion stretches out from the cave's mouth I *clockwise, from top left* sketch; plan; view of structure from below; view out over surrounding landscape

# STEVEN HOLL
# NELSON-ATKINS MUSEUM OF ART EXPANSION

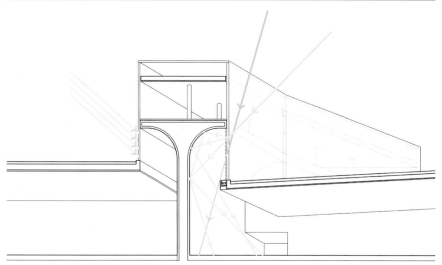

Faced with the task of expanding a monumental cultural institution with views over a formal sculpture garden in Kansas City, Steven Holl decided to work through deference and difference. He placed the new galleries and entrance alongside the existing museum and partially under the terraces of the sculpture garden. The addition is one long building that houses connected galleries, but which appears in the landscape as a series of transparent and translucent "crystals." Thus, the formal enclosure of art makes way for an episodic and participatory emphasis on the museum experience.

*left* gallery space I *top left* cross section of the gallery wall I *top right* model I *opposite* interior spaces

Deep inside the Swiss Alps a science-fiction world hums away. Four giant alternators sit buried in a cave whose surfaces are covered with granite, glass, steel and polymer, denying all sense of the rough forces of geology and hydrology that allow this plant to produce electricity. The sculptural doors, maws of concrete with translucent glass panels, are the only evidence to the outside world of the plant's existence.

*left* **doors to the plant** | *below left* **axonometric** | *opposite* **interior views**

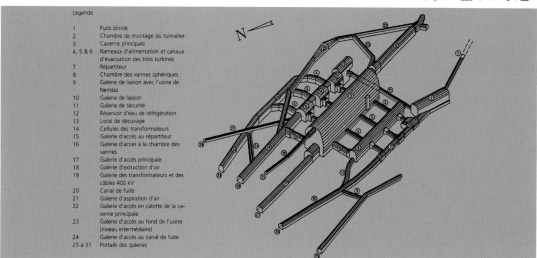

Légende

| | |
|---|---|
| 1 | Puits blindé |
| 2 | Chambre de montage du tunnelier |
| 3 | Caverne principale |
| 4, 5 & 6 | Rameaux d'alimentation et canaux d'évacuation des trois turbines |
| 7 | Répartiteur |
| 8 | Chambre des vannes sphériques |
| 9 | Galerie de liaison avec l'usine de Nendaz |
| 10 | Galerie de liaison |
| 11 | Galerie de sécurité |
| 12 | Réservoir d'eau de réfrigération |
| 13 | Local de décuvage |
| 14 | Cellules des transformateurs |
| 15 | Galerie d'accès au répartiteur |
| 16 | Galerie d'accès à la chambre des vannes |
| 17 | Galerie d'accès principale |
| 18 | Galerie d'extraction d'air |
| 19 | Galerie des transformateurs et des câbles 400 kV |
| 20 | Canal de fuite |
| 21 | Galerie d'aspiration d'air |
| 22 | Galerie d'accès en calotte de la caverne principale |
| 23 | Galerie d'accès au fond de l'usine (niveau intermédiaire) |
| 24 | Galerie d'accès au canal de fuite |
| 25 à 31 | Portails des galeries |

# CLAUDINE LORENZ, FLORIAN MUSSO
# HYDROELECTRIC PLANT

# 3

# Unfolding the Land
Opening up the earth to create architectural forms

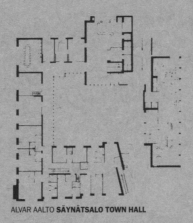

ALVAR AALTO **SÄYNÄTSALO TOWN HALL**

FRANK LLOYD WRIGHT **FALLINGWATER**

Architecture can unfold the earth. Plates tilt up, fissures appear; what were once caves are now rooms with views. Ground narrows into ramps that curve up toward the sky or dive down into the earth. Smooth finishes replace rough rock, glass lets light in above eye level, and what is inside and what is outside becomes confused as horizontal planes move past each other. In place of façades indicating the hidden interior world, or roofs standing against the horizon to shelter the interior, space spirals up from or down into the ground, blurring the distinction between what is below and what is above, what is a solid base and what is shelter.[1]

Architecture that unfolds the earth destabilizes some of the most fundamental aspects of canonical architecture. If the Ecole des Beaux-Arts taught us that all buildings of any importance should organize themselves according to a geometric division of spatial cells, with hierarchical importance given to central functions, it also believed that this organization should have a face to the outside world that was inflected by those distributions. The building should in the end subject itself to an autonomous system of representation. This was one of the benchmarks of the neo-classical system as it was developed in Paris and spread throughout the world. A building's central axis should lead from its heart directly to its most important function. Along the way, a system—invisible to anyone but the architect and which should include rules for everything from the way a cornice effects a visual transition from wall to ceiling to the kind of order that is appropriate for different spaces—would calibrate all that we could experience.[2]

Modernism modified this system's language, going so far as to argue for broken and fractured organizations and façades that were purposefully off-center or even blank. However, the movement remained true to the Beaux-Arts idea that a building

should be laid out according to the rational arrangement of the site's program. This meant that a building's façades needed to be in keeping with an established style or system of representation. Buildings would always have façades, main axes and organizational systems that would relate to each other. We have now developed buildings that often frustrate such clean dictates—shopping malls, for instance, which usually have no façades, revolve around multiple centers, and are purposefully meandering and confusing—making these architectural dreams seem grandiose and pertaining only to the realm of high art. A generation of architects is beginning to make buildings that question these clean relationships and replace them with a new order that is less clear and more intriguing.

There are, of course, roots for such attitudes. Alvar Aalto's Säynätsalo Town Hall (1948, 1950–52) is a good example: a civic center whose core is not the meeting hall, but an open courtyard. The central space is open to one side, leaking out toward the surrounding forest and moving up from the ground plane via a series of grass steps until it becomes the *piano nobile*, the ceremonial "first floor" around which all major functions should be organized. The library, however, is on the ground floor. The main door to the complex is in a corner on that same lower level. Entering here or by ascending the grass steps at the back, visitors move around and up in hallways and terraces to the council chamber. It is a dim room that slopes upward, but not to light. It is a piece of the earth, a cave, lifted up at the end of a spiraling motion. The Säynätsalo building does not have a clear front, center or ground plane, but visitors achieve a sense of the heart of the building through the exploration and unfolding of the ground. Although Aalto's forms have often been copied by architects, this complex organizational form does not seem to have had a great deal

of influence. Hints of its complexity are apparent in the work of James Stirling, and in countless small community centers in Scandinavian countries. Perhaps it was too radical in its disavowal of centralized and clearly legible form to be imitated more frequently.

Aalto himself has explored this same idea in numerous buildings, including several houses. His work found a parallel in that of Frank Lloyd Wright (1867–1959), who also began exploring the notion of unfolding the land in several of his later buildings. The Guggenheim Museum in New York (1943–46, 1956–59) is a prime example of his thinking at its most radical: in place of a building with a façade and a central axis, it is a spiral that rises up from the pavement to become the gallery space and the façade at the same time. It leaves a top-heavy spindle stuck in Manhattan's grid and a central atrium of dizzying proportions. The building's only failing is that it does not disappear into the mists so much as it just ends without effectively penetrating the ground. It is only a literal spiral.

In some of his housing projects, Lloyd Wright took the idea of unfolding the earth further. While he is famous for defying natural conditions with such homes as Fallingwater in Bear Run, Pennsylvania (1935–39), he claimed to be interested in building with the land.[3] In his design for the Johnson House in Wisconsin (1947), he turned his architecture into a set of parallel lines emerging from the landscape. However, he succumbed to the urge to make form, cracking open the horizontal layering with which he began the design. The order of horizontal and vertical elements took over the smooth spiraling of spaces into each other.

It was some of Lloyd Wright's more eccentric pupils who took his "organic" notions to their logical extension. Bruce Goff (1904–82) especially delighted in designing spirals. His Joe Price House and Studio in Bartlesville,

BRUCE GOFF **JOE PRICE HOUSE AND STUDIO**

JOHN LAUTNER **ARANGO RESIDENCE**

Oklahoma (1956–74) retains a sense of the earth with roofs made of coal, but also begins to look like a wigwam erected on the planes. Rocks and machine-made materials mix in free compositions, water animates the space, and what center there is becomes lost in the complexity of the house's curves.[4]

Several of Goff's followers have delved further into the ground to make modern-day sod huts. Others, such as the eccentric Los Angeles architect John Lautner (a student of Wright's), have made a revelation of the topography the starting point of their smoothly undulating designs. In Silvertop: Reiner-Burchill Residence (1956–74), the hilltop mansion Lautner designed in Los Angeles, the path up the hill takes a hairpin turn into the heart of the house. Here, two low-flying ovoid shapes hover just above the ground, opening up what appears to be a vast space made even larger because, without supports to interrupt the arc of glass, the walls recede completely from view. The ground plane becomes a weightless slab whose lines abstract the surrounding hills. Bedrooms and ancillary spaces are much more cavelike in their containment, looking as if they have been hewn out of the site's rock.

This sense of exhilarating freedom from cracking open the earth becomes even more joyous in the Arango Residence Lautner designed in Acapulco (1973). The roof is a boomerang-shaped sunshade jutting out from the side of a steep cliff, once again opening the cave to a view that overwhelms the space and goes on into infinity. Below the living floor, Lautner surrounded a patio with a swimming pool that traces the edges of the site. The swimmer can follow the geology of the site (both man-made and natural) with the rhythm of her or his strokes. Sea and rock come together at a point that can actually be inhabited.

Although Lautner's forms seem flamboyant and later in his life became more and more extreme (serving as backdrops for such James Bond movies as *Goldfinger*), they only brought out Lloyd Wright's tendency to match the grandeur of nature with a human line. Slicing open the ground, both architects sought to make the wound of construction in the earth. Instead of a roof placed over a vertical structure, an abstraction of the earth opens up a new realm underneath its gravity-defying presence.[5]

What most architects lack today is the hubris this attitude evokes. Building these flying saucers that hug a new ground plane often means clearing the site and pouring a great deal of concrete. All interior forms, therefore, are restricted by the work that must be done to support this gesture, becoming abstract and primitive caves that are more suited to extreme living situations. It is perhaps no accident that most of these houses exist on the edges of occupiable land, where their cliff-side sites justify such moves at the boundary of what we might call architecture.

In contrast to such bold actions, most architects try to make more complex and tentative adaptations and reactions to the landscape. While New Mexico–based architect Antoine Predock has made a few hillside houses that pick up on Wrightian motifs, his most successful work has been in the public realm. He made his name with the Nelson Fine Arts Center in Tempe (1985–89), where the cave is at the heart of the building, but is not immediately apparent. A central axis penetrates all the way through the structure's heart toward this space, but once there, the building does not lay itself out neatly. Instead, the courtyard is a place of shadows over which rises a triangular roof. Filled with columns, the space is a maze through which it is difficult to find the way toward the museum and other functions. The roof does not mark the

end of the building, but transforms itself into an outdoor auditorium from which viewers can watch films projected onto the adjacent indoor theater's fly tower. The whole building has the sense of being somewhere between the massiveness of a mesa and the fragmented, specific massing of a functional structure. Predock has made an artificial mountain, hollowed it out to contain a cave, and then fissured and occupied the building so that the analogy begins to break down as the building breaks open.

In more recent buildings, Predock has continued these types of investigations. The American Heritage Center and Art Museum (1986–93, see p. 128) he designed at the University of Wyoming is more clearly a mountain with a cave at the heart, but such structures as the Student Center at the University of California at Santa Cruz (1998) and the Social Sciences and Humanities Building at the University of California at Davis (1999) are more ambivalent. Both exist as cuts into the earth, out of which jagged profiles zigzag their way toward the sky. Paths lead through, around and over parts of each building. Visitors do not have a clear sense of where the original ground was, finding themselves lost in a modern labyrinth.

Predock likes to think of his buildings as excavations mirroring the layers one finds in road cuts in America's west: starting with the most ancient forms of rock at the base, finding a few strange animal skeletons in higher levels, and ending with the detritus of human civilization, from beer cans to newspapers, at the top. In this way, the architect believes he can make buildings that do not show a contradiction but rather a continuity between ground and human construction. He then solidifies this relationship into as simple and strong a shape as he can muster. At its most extreme, it would be a "landscraper": a triangular form jutting out from the

ABALOS + HERREROS **CASA VERDE**

ZAHA HADID **TRAM TERMINAL**

ground and containing all the building's functions. In his Spencer Theater in the New Mexico desert (1994–97, see p. 116), Predock almost achieved the monumental clarity of this gesture as he was able to shape the building into a single triangular form that lifted up off the flat desert floor.[6]

Two very different houses reduce this method to a domestic scale. Stanley Saitowitz's DiNapoli House of 1992, in Sarasota, California, consists of parallel rectangles arranged along a long ridge. Each rectangle appears to be an independent element, as if an earthquake has separated the house into a set of units. Saitowitz heightens the theme of shifting through the circulation element, which slips in-between the volumes and down a set of stairs that move from outside into a courtyard and then into the house, widening as they descend the slope. These elongated lines dissolve into vast living spaces that are all open to each other. A skeleton of intersecting structural elements admits light from every angle and at differing heights. The inhabitant is suspended on the shifting planes, a new realm where nothing is static and enclosed. The occupiable rooftop celebrates this accomplishment with balconies that abstract the terraced site and let the owners enjoy a view of Californian suburbia.

The second residence is Casa Verde near Madrid (1997, see p. 110) by Spanish firm Abalos + Herreros, where nature is abstracted into a grid of concrete blocks with grass growing in-between them. The house's form is determined by the ramp-like adjacent garden, which takes a hairpin turn to become the residence's roof. Windows pop in and out of the green monolith, eating into its abstraction and making it habitable.

Not all such landscrapers have a domestic scale. Berlin-based architect Daniel Libeskind has always focused on

unearthing the suppressed memories and realities of our urban condition, but he has also become interested in unfolding the site to turn it into a spiral rising above the ground. His first move in this direction is apparent in Berlin's Jewish Museum (1988–99). The museum does not even have a front door; visitors enter through a tunnel from the Museum of Berlin History. A labyrinth of angular forms spreads out in front of visitors, culminating in the tall space of memory. In this silent and dark concrete vault, attention turns upward, away from the subterranean place of reflection to which visitors have descended. Finding their way back through the twisting corridors, they climb a grand staircase to the *piano nobile* where the main exhibition spaces are located. However, the building never assembles itself as an object placed on the ground; there is no center, no shaping of the space, no articulation of construction. The building is a pure extrusion of the jagged line Libeskind made in the land, its sides glistening in a metal coat as if they have been mined rather than built up.

Throughout the 1990s, Libeskind explored this way of building in such designs as the Felix Nussbaum Haus in Osnabrück, Germany (1995–98). He also interpreted the urban landscape as a ground that he could incise, add on to and extrapolate, but never fully escape. His architecture was a way of mining memory as it existed in the previous marks humans had made on the land and a way of building up these traces into voids that were inhabitable and essentially empty of anything other than what has not yet happened or what could happen in the future.

In his proposal for the addition to the Victoria & Albert Museum in London, Libeskind has moved out of the ground and wrapped his extrusions around themselves. Spirals of interconnected spaces uncoil the site into a set of linked

tubular environments. The spaces support each other, and the building's skin looks like the scales of a snake raised to strike an unknown target. Architecture is a self-sufficient monster that unfolds toward and through an emptiness that Libeskind decides not to portray with all the panoply of construction elements.[7]

A similar strategy of abstraction—though it comes from very different impulses—is pursued by London-based architect Zaha Hadid. Her work stems from the teachings of the Architectural Association in London, and was initially inspired by her collaborations with Rem Koolhaas, seeking to incorporate the excitement of metropolitan life into forms whose complexity turns them into magic mountains. In more recent years, she has abandoned this strategy to concentrate on a path of formal exploration. The two dominant forms in her work are now the bundle and the spiral: a fluid arrangement of spaces that either exists as parallel, overlapping and snake-like tubes hugging the ground, or as a continuous shape unfolding from the ground and reaching up toward the top of the building. In place of skyscrapers or "event structures," she proposes pathways that open out into buildings.

Pathways are themselves spatial elaborations of simple planes. In Hadid's latest buildings, and most evident in her pavilion for the Landesgartenschau in Weil am Rhein (1999, see p. 122), the visitor inhabits a continuous set of planes that are without walls, the definers of interior and exterior space. The pavilion is a curved structure defined by a bending ramp that rises up in the middle to shelter meeting and exhibition rooms before descending again to the ground. What is most remarkable about this building is the lack of any kind of cellular division: the spaces inside are continuous, their separate functions indicated by changes

ENRIC MIRALLES AND CARME PINÓS **ARCHERY RANGE**

in level or their relative size. Bands of windows serve not to penetrate the structure but to emphasize the layered quality of the pavilion as a whole.

Hadid goes further than almost any architect in realizing the landscraper as the unfolding and opening up of the land. She has not done so by literally elongating or reproducing the basic plane on which we stand, but by seeing space as the empty abstraction it is. The void is not the result of enclosure by external structure but the generator of form. What surfaces it produces are the minimal skins that flow from its needs, elaborated to effect a sense of layering and transition between the different parts of the interior and the exterior. Here, architecture is like a robe unfurling from a dance of spatial implications, blurring the distinction between what the architect makes and what we can only assume was there before.[8]

Against these fluid structures—whether they are lines cut into the earth to open up new caves, or spatial voids creating a new ground plane that is unidentifiable from a pre-existing condition—stand those landscrapers that clearly distinguish themselves from the land. The cracking open of the land reveals whole new topologies, like a geode showing an interior of crystalline formations, although in many cases these buildings are much rougher than the smooth exteriors would suggest. The buildings' almost primitive forms use their sunken state to argue for a more basic formal language.

Many architects who build these types of structures have gained inspiration from the work of Italian modernist architect Carlo Scarpa (1906–78), especially his design for the Brion Family Cemetery near Treviso in Italy (1969–78). For the cemetery, Scarpa amalgamated many of the forms he had developed for other projects. He took the entrance

to the architecture school of Venice, where walls unfold from the paving and the paving itself almost becomes the building or pieces of it, and married it with the cave-like design for the Casa Ottolenghi (1974–79), a house that develops as fragments of rooms from an entrance terrace that is also the roof. The house's many walls and piers are covered with planting, so that it practically disappears into the surrounding vegetation. Inside, small pieces of marble form the honorific frames for mantels and mirrors. Domesticity falls apart into instances of order within the cave.

In Treviso, Scarpa sliced and raised up the earth, transforming it into concrete layers whose corners turn into dense essays on construction itself. Scarpa controls axes with such elements as a row of cypress trees and a fountain. The cemetery's one masterful moment is a low arch over the sarcophagi of the patriarch and matriarch. This concrete form is also a bridge planted with grass. It opens up a space in the earth, and serves as a moment of stillness around which the axes of this complicated design turn.[9]

One of the most influential structures to delaminate the earth since the cemetery is the Archery Range Catalan architects Enric Miralles (1955–2000) and Carme Pinós designed for the Barcelona Olympic Games (1989–92, see p. 126). Facing a field in a valley leading out of the town proper, the facility is no more than a fractured façade in front of a set of locker rooms and offices. The major part of the building's face is a perforated and leaning concrete wall whose top folds back into the structure while its bottom lifts off the ground. The exterior is reduced to its most basic function as a shield (which is also a clue to the structure's function), made clear when the long line of the retaining wall breaks down into a set of angled segments following the valley's serrated edge. At the entrance, a canopy of triangular fragments takes the long parallel lines

that form the building's roof and crumples them into a ceremonial welcome. The building thus represents the topographical lines on the site that the architect has wilfully manipulated to make space and then faced with a set of defensive shields.

The interior is not a great sweep of space, but a collection of triangular and irregular environments across which a concrete roof, punctuated by skylights, runs counter to the general circulation pattern. Light comes through the perforated shields and washes along the curved walls of the changing rooms. Spiky protuberances of walls knit together inside and outside. The Archery Range is not so much one space as it is a set of moves, digs, cuts and planes whose complexity defines a particular and peculiar order. Instead of the smooth unfolding of the land, Pinós and Miralles hint at the ritualistic violence that shoots out from the cave into the land. The duo went on to build another landscraper, Igualada Cemetery (see p. 76), in Barcelona in 1993, and Carme Pinós has gone on to incise the ground with forms that become more and more undulating in such projects as the Market for the JVC Project in Guadalajara. Low walls and arching bridges create rows where stalls can be placed and people can circulate while still feeling as if they are exploring the contours of the land on which the grid exists.

New York–based architects Tod Williams and Billie Tsien are masters of creating intricate topologies that shoot out from the land to propose a blurred and complex border between the man-made and the natural, forming what is, in the end, a whole new terrain. The studio has two main interests: first, in representing circulation as the major element that gives life to and lets us explore a building; second, in the tectonics that dissolve the distinction between surface and structure into a continuous weaving

TOD WILLIAMS AND BILLIE TSIEN **CRANBROOK NATATORIUM**

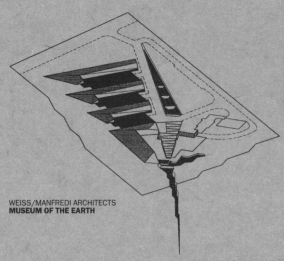

WEISS/MANFREDI ARCHITECTS
**MUSEUM OF THE EARTH**

of construction. With these points in mind, Williams and Tsien created a number of low and ground-hugging buildings, such as the dormitories at the University of Virginia of 1995, which explore the nature of a sloping topography (especially in the commons building), and the Phoenix Museum of Art (1991–94), which dissolves a civic structure into an almost anonymous layering of ramps that turns into gallery spaces. In three more recent projects in the u.s.—the Neurosciences Institute in La Jolla, California (1992–96, see p. 118), the Cranbrook Natatorium in Michigan (1996–2000), and the Johns Hopkins University Student Art Center in Baltimore (2001)—Williams and Tsien have reconfigured the ground to make new places and to more clearly engage the earth.

The Neurosciences Institute comprises three parts: an arch of laboratories set into a cliff, an auditorium closing the courtyard formed by the concave curve of the laboratories, and an administration building sailing off the cliff. The heart of the complex is fractured by the architects' desire to work with the site itself; it may be the work that goes on there, which is to say underground, or the void of the courtyard, or the auditorium, a cavernous splay of space used for recitals and research discussions. These three parts flow from each other and none has its own center. The laboratories move out from the cliff to the sun, the courtyard curves around to allow for circulation, and the auditorium opens up toward the stage. The architects cut through these overlapping elements with ramps and other circulation devices, and the composition's fragmentary divisions are rendered as leaning walls. Glass and concrete move past each other, unveiling bits of the interior and allowing entry.

The institute does not have an overall shape. It is an extension of the cliff that is open-ended, allowing the user to move through a set of open spaces. Along the way, she or he experiences a collage of different elements that begin to establish a new language of architectural connections and covering. The administration building finally glides off the cliff, its farthest point a glass cockpit where the director surveys his domain. This gesture of confidence, removal and control is the weakest point of what is otherwise a building whose strength comes from its unfolding of the site.

Cranbrook Natatorium is a simpler space. Set into the ground on the eastern edge of Eliel Saarinen's campus of stone and brick buildings, the pool masks its large volume within a slope of the land. Its large roof does not interfere with the complex composition of the original campus, but offers an intermediary between the rhythm of Saarinen's courtyards and the open sweep of the athletic fields. One enters the building as into a cave, down and into darkness, to find a simple box surmounted by two conical skylights. Low-set bands of windows continue the space out into the adjacent playing fields.

Similarly, at Johns Hopkins University Student Art Center, Williams and Tsien use the slope of the land to create an open space. However, in this case, as in the Neurosciences Institute, the space takes the form of a courtyard. The two major blocks of offices and meeting rooms line the courtyard, leaving only a narrow passage out at one end. While the building's ground level is low and designed to visually continue the land, the second story floats freely above and is an essay in modernist abstraction. Outdoor balconies turn the lower floors into plinths for these upper-level spaces, while ramps connect them down to the structure and weave the whole complex back together. Williams and Tsien have formed a seamless web of architecture, and it is hard to tell what is existing ground and what is new land.

In a similar vein, New York firm Weiss/Manfredi Architects has designed the Museum of the Earth in Ithaca, New York (see p. 114). The main building opens out onto a path that descends the hill past several large berms. These berms catch and funnel storm run-off, making the building an elaboration of the natural eco-system. The museum's clear-span structure flips open to permit views past this unfolding landscape to the repetitive forms of the surrounding hills.

Perhaps the most impressive of the recent unfolding buildings is Diamond Ranch High School near Pomona in California (1999–2000, see p. 112), designed by Thom Mayne of Morphosis. The building is a direct unfolding of the land. It started as a "cut-and-fill" operation that re-formed the hillside into terraces used as playing fields. The school is just one of these terraces, cut through lengthwise to allow students to enter its spaces and to let light into the finger-like classroom buildings. The buildings' roofs result from Mayne's interpretation of the existing site's contours into a pattern of geometric abstractions. They fold this way and that, breaking down the bulk of the 2,000-student school into what appear to be the fractured folds of a land shaped by earthquakes—which is of course what lurks underneath the seemingly smooth surfaces of these hills. The folds are also elongations and enlargements of the roofscape of endlessly repeated single-family homes around the school.

The school's central axis is a narrow canyon between these buildings. It twists and turns its way across the site, occasionally opening up to views of the valley below. Such major elements as the library and the gymnasium grow out of this landscape to become important civic areas. Their structure, which made possible this elaboration of space into functional rooms, finally reveals itself as thin branches in the form of trusses that hold up what seems to be a weightless

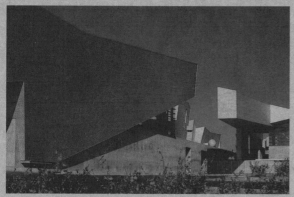
MORPHOSIS **DIAMOND RANCH HIGH SCHOOL**

roof. These large and light areas culminate the public spaces Morphosis has dug out of the hill. In return for the site it replaces, Diamond Ranch offers a set of public spaces, from the playing fields above and below, to the almost medieval street at the project's heart, and to the cave-like places of gathering. Unfolding the land leads to a common appreciation of a place transformed in a manner that a whole community can occupy and understand.

Against such a fractured aesthetic stands a group of buildings that presents more ordered versions of the cave opening up to the light. The most magnificent example is Mecanoo's library at Delft University of Technology (1992–97, see p. 108). Faced with having the monumental Van den Broek and Bakema campus center next to their site, the architects decided to hide their library below a carpet of grass that slopes up gently from the ground to a point where students can survey the whole campus and surrounding fields. The building can be understood as a lifting up of the meadows, crisscrossed by irrigation ditches, that form the basic unit of Dutch landscape design. A conical tower rises up from the platform as if it were a church steeple, by which traditionally people would recognize the presence of a village within the otherwise flat continuum of meadows.

The library's interior is mainly given over to one vast reading room, and the focal point is a wall of books. One glass wall looks out to the campus, and another through a computer room to the surroundings. Painted blue, the structure represents the essence of a library, even if most of the books are stored in compact cases in the basement. The huge room from which students view this display of erudition is open, pierced only by the tower's base. Inside the cone, reading "circles" spiral up and nearly penetrate through the grass under which most of the building hides. The architects believe they have designed a library that is closer to the gathering spaces found at airports or convention centers than those in places of learning. With the advent of computers, and the need for ecologically sensitive design, they point out, built space becomes an open entity that has to be fed by technology but is not filled with anything. Freedom opened up within the earth has to be designed as a liberating potential and not a leftover, a task Mecanoo has accomplished.

German firm Behnisch, Behnisch & Partner pursued similar goals in the 1998 design for the Institute for Forestry and Nature Research in Wageningen, the Netherlands (see p. 120). The architects brought nature into courtyards and onto the roof. In fact, nature worms its way in and out of the building, leaving the glass and metal assemblies and a few planes of wood as examples of a former order that is being eaten away by the very force the institute is meant to study.

In Europe, stringent regulations demand that architects find ways of building that are considerably more energy efficient than traditional stylistic disciplines. For this reason, the use of grass roofs has become quite common, especially in northern Europe. The small Educational Television building designed by Dutch firm MVRDV in 1997 is a good example of a structure that appears from one angle (the down slope) to be an object, but from the opposite angle (the up slope) disappears below a grass plane that seems to continue the ground on which visitors are standing. There is an element of camouflage in many of these buildings, but the need for one or more walls to let light and warmth in and to offer views out also allows a double reading.

An even more fundamental reversal of ground and ceiling in a library makes Dominique Perrault's Bibliothèque Nationale de France in Paris (1995) so successful. Although Perrault has never argued that his building is a direct response to environ-mental conditions, his fascination with an architecture that recovers and encloses some sense (however artificial) of nature has been constant in his work. In earlier designs, such as the Usinor-Sacilor Conference Center of 1991 in Saint-Germain-en-Laye, he chose to bury his work and continue the design of a garden over its top, while in the Paris library he created an artificial nature. Perrault buried the building's main bulk in a plinth on which he placed four glass towers. Shaped like open books, the towers are used for storage and put learning on display as isolated fragments of human technology. What we do with them is base reality. After visitors have mounted the broad steps to the place where they would expect the superstructure of reading areas to exist, they find out that these towers are inaccessible symbols. Visitors have to descend four levels to what Perrault terms the "jardin sacré," a forest transplanted from Normandy at the building's heart. Reading rooms surround this piece of nature, bringing the idea of learning back to the notion of the "academy" as a grove of trees where scholars would gather to learn as in ancient Athens.

Nature as something that gives force and context to the acquisition of knowledge is an intellectual and spatial idea in this library and in the one at Delft. Swiss practice Décosterd & Rahm's project for a gymnasium outside Grenoble (1999–2000) responds directly to the body as well as the mind. Outwardly a deceptively simple block disguised to appear as if it were part of nature, inside the gym's response to nature goes much deeper. A wall of glass acts as a greenhouse in which plants grow. They live on the carbon dioxide and sweat produced by the gymnasts as they exercise in the main hall, while supplying oxygen for their bodies to consume. The whole structure builds on the firm's earlier experiments with spaces that dissolve into the intrinsic cycles of the body and nature.

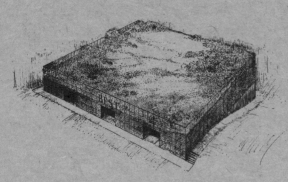

SITE **BEST STORE**

SITE **BEST STORE**

Europe is not the only place where architects are investigating buildings that respond directly to environmental conditions and nature. As early as 1983, architect Kevin Roche designed an entire factory whose roof, though not a garden, was conceived of as a new ground plane. The Cummins Engine Company in Columbus, Indiana presents a low line to the road. In contrast to the curving contours of the entry area, this concrete oasis in the middle of a forest resembles a paved parterre in a French garden. Drivers swing by a pond set in a landscape of reclaimed nature, then rise up to a parking area that is in actuality the factory's roof. Inside, a continuous line of windows set at eye level presents the workers with a view of the forest floor. Lost in nature while they are producing engines, the mechanics are like primeval metal smiths whose anvils glow in a dark wilderness.

The architects and artists who have grouped themselves together as SITE (Sculpture in the Environment) are master designers of buildings that extend nature and seek to make us aware of the technology we apply to the world to open up a space of habitation within it. Led by James Wines in New York, the designers have been developing since 1970 a method of making buildings that reverses the "machine in the garden" metaphor by putting the garden in, over and through the machine.[10] Throughout the 1980s, they designed stores for the Best Corporation, each one a variation on the theme of how nature might enter into and even dissolve a commercial space. Some early façades crumbled or came apart, as if they had been abandoned, while the stores they proposed for Northern California in the late 1980s would have been invaded by nature or would have disappeared completely underground. The construction grid and shelves would have been the corset for a vegetation run wild. At that time, however, the Best company had fallen on hard times, so Wines and his colleagues applied their thinking to other projects, such as the unbuilt Terrarium Building, whose façade is a display case for nature. In another example, SITE suggests that nature enters the Forest Building store in Richmond, Virginia. Walking along an aisle the shopper comes to a fissure in the ground and ceiling where a sliver of nature appears. After traversing this interruption, the shopper continues into the store's air-conditioned and fluorescent world.

The legacy of SITE's neo-nature and other architects' opening of the earth to reveal caves remain as prototypes for a new nature in which the stable ground for construction and the myth of an inviolate nature will disappear in favor of an architecture that in its very instability and strangeness encourages new kinds of spatial exploration and experience. By counterfeiting nature and by exploring its internal fissures we begin to construct an architecture that is as real as nature itself.

# ZAHA HADID
# TRAM TERMINAL

At the edge of Strasbourg lines converge: highway on- and off-ramps, bus lines and a tramway. London-based architect Zaha Hadid has added another set of lines. Sharp diagonals guide cars and passengers toward a place where steel columns, leaning this way and that, strain to push up canopies and sheltering walls. It is here that commuters wait for public transportation to take them into the heart of the city. Minimal in its enclosed volumes, this is an expression of infrastructure turning into place.

**opposite** tramlines cut through the center of the terminal

**above and right** covered waiting areas for passengers

**top right** a road skirts the terminal

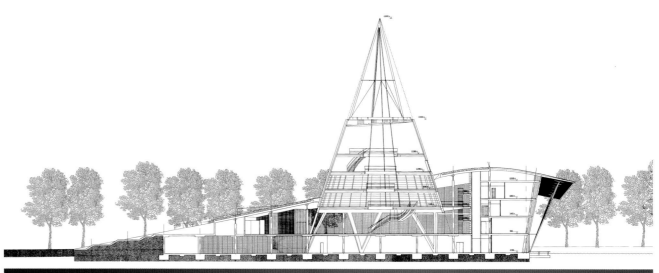

# MECANOO
# CENTRAL
# LIBRARY

The premise that information is becoming increasingly suppressed and controlled when it should be more and more accessible and democratic was the starting point for Mecanoo's design for a library at Delft Technical University, the Netherlands. The books are stored in dense stacks, while the reading room is a luminous space modeled on an airport terminal. A sloping grass plane, the roof continues and terminates the campus area, also recalling the meadow that was once on the building's site. A cone-shaped tower protrudes through this new ground to signal and anchor the place of knowledge.

*opposite, clockwise from top right* long section through conical tower and central hall; canted glass walls form three of the building's façades I *above* the library roof extends the landscape I *right* interior view of the cone's base

# ABALOS + HERREROS
## CASA VERDE

Envisioned as a "green machine," this house for a landscape architect was to have been constructed on the edge of Madrid where the sprawling metropolis confronts what remains of pine forests and streams. The design is a collection of simple, geometric forms, partially covered by vegetation and set into the slope. It does not so much conform to the existing topography as it re-proposes it to provide the owner with views and living space. Architecture, here, is a form of three-dimensional gardening.

*opposite* sketch | *top, middle and bottom* digital renderings with views to the city in the distance | *bottom right* front [top] and back [bottom] elevations

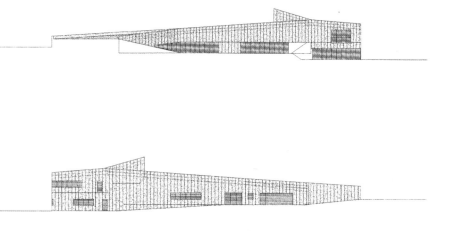

# MORPHOSIS
# DIAMOND RANCH
# HIGH SCHOOL

A steep hillside coupled with the demands for parking and playing fields made a set of terraces the answer for this project in Pomona, California. Rather than placing an object on one of these steps, architect Thom Mayne continued the contour lines of the natural setting to form roofs beneath which he housed the classrooms. Streets wind up the hills into the surrounding suburban landscape. Between the classrooms, Mayne cut a canyonlike gathering space for the academic oasis.

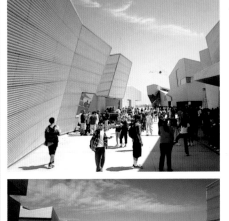

*above and right* street views | *left* view from playing fields | *opposite* ground-level perspective

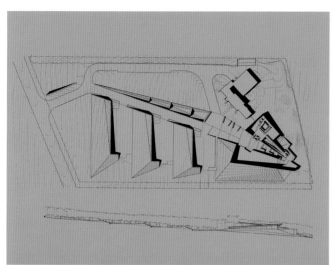

# WEISS/MANFREDI ARCHITECTS
# MUSEUM OF THE EARTH

Commissioned to design a museum that houses an extensive paleontological collection, Weiss/Manfredi Architects devised a structure that has several levels buried in the land. The parking lot is subsumed by the earth, above which an interactive research gallery barely registers on the surface of the land. The two buildings that do rise above the newly constituted ground—a public education hall and an exhibition facility—mimic the sinuous geology of the Fingers Lake region of America in which the project is located.

*opposite* sketch | *clockwise, from top left* site plan; models

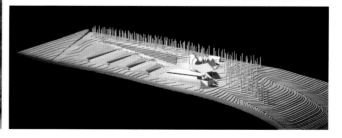

After drawing and modeling several versions of his "landscraper," Albuquerque-based architect Antoine Predock finally built one as a community theater in Ruidoso, New Mexico. The white, limestone-clad form rises up off the flat New Mexico plane to gesture toward the often snow-covered peaks behind it. The building's faceted shape makes it as complex as the surrounding mountains, although its overall impression of mass is reduced by the incisions into the building to allow light to enter. Through one of these cuts, a glass crystalline shape bursts out of one side to house the public lobby. All other functions are suppressed into this civic sculpture at the scale of the landscape.

*left* public lobby | *below* site plan | *opposite, top* front façade | *opposite, bottom* view from base of steps

# ANTOINE PREDOCK
## SPENCER THEATER

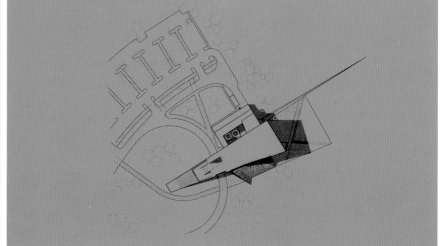

# TOD WILLIAMS AND BILLIE TSIEN
# NEUROSCIENCES INSTITUTE

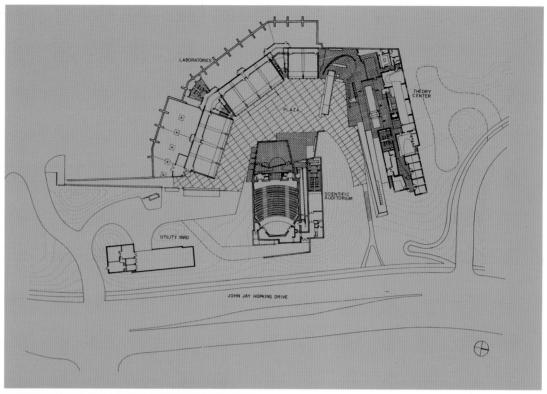

While the nearby Salk Institute (Louis I. Kahn) in La Jolla, California proclaimed the importance of science in two fingers gesturing out to the ocean, Williams and Tsien chose to bury their laboratories for the neurological research center into the hillside. They left a canted wall of glass to face a concave courtyard, the center of which is occupied by an auditorium, also sunk into the hillside. Only the administrative offices, housed in a simple and thin rectangle, sail away from this earthbound world.

*opposite* the theory center points inland from the Pacific
*left* courtyard | *top left* entrance to the auditorium
*top right* site plan

Taking a sensible and sensuous attitude toward environmental concerns for an agency that wanted to highlight its commitment to sustainable uses of nature, the German firm designed a building where almost all the work spaces are naturally ventilated. By arranging the offices (Wageningen, the Netherlands) in bars between two gardens, Behnisch, Behnisch & Partner has created three thin fingers between buffer areas that provide thermal insulation. The architects chose off-the-shelf components to complement their logical approach to site arrangements, going so far as to use only short lengths of wood, thereby using in a more efficient manner the trees the institute is trying to preserve.

*clockwise, from top* **plan; sixty-five percent of the building's outer walls are made from clear glass; each office opens onto one of the gardens; local wood was used to reduce transport costs |** *opposite* **the garden is used as an extension of the workplace**

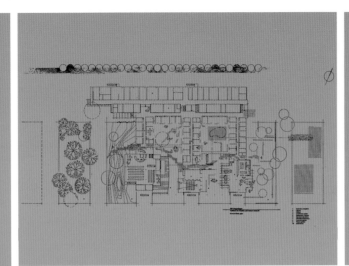

# BEHNISCH, BEHNISCH & PARTNER
## INSTITUTE FOR FORESTRY AND NATURE RESEARCH

# ZAHA HADID
# LANDESGARTENSCHAU
# PAVILION

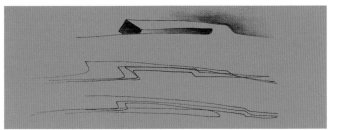

Paths bundle together to form a building in this small pavilion Hadid designed as part of a national garden exhibition in Weil-am-Rhein, Germany. The main circulation path around the park rises up off the ground to become the mass, covered with parallel lines of planters and other green areas, underneath which shelters a small exhibition area. There are no straight walls or little boxes, only the continuous curves of path, wall and roof that carve out a space from the lines of movement.

*opposite, top* sketch | *opposite, bottom* wood-clad offices sit next to the concrete exhibition space *clockwise, from top left* staircase at the pavilion's center; aerial view from the south side; exterior view at dusk; interior concrete bridge

# GUSTAV PEICHL
# SATELLITE TRACKING STATION

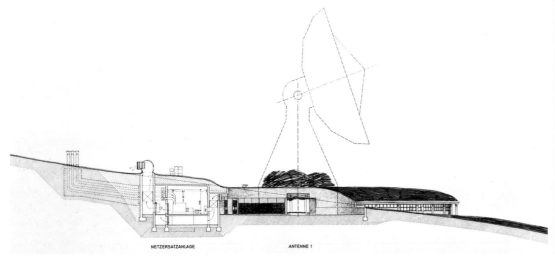

NETZERSATZANLAGE          ANTENNE 1

Due to its beautiful and protected natural surroundings, the bulk of this sophisticated tracking station is underground. Only a few façades, which recall local vernacular farm buildings, peek out of the steeply sloped site in Styria, Austria. A circular courtyard creates a controlled counterpoint to the undulating spaces around the complex. The giant dish becomes a piece of abstract culture that floats up out of what appears to be undisturbed nature.

*top left* the station is firmly planted into the hillside I *top right and opposite* aerial views
*left* long section

# ENRIC MIRALLES AND CARME PINÓS

## ARCHERY RANGE

Recalling both military fortifications and roadworks, the facility was constructed for the 1992 Olympic Games in Barcelona. Competition spaces appear as a set of fragments, as sharp as arrowheads, dancing in and out of an undulating line that faces an open field. The roofs and retaining walls of the main building are a continuation of the contours of this artificial tableland in the hills above Barcelona.

*opposite* concrete façade panels with triangular cut-outs | *above* the disjointed concrete roof panels are connected by zinc scuppers | *right* cross section

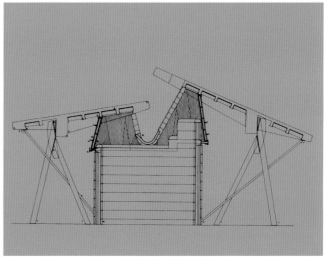

# ANTOINE PREDOCK
# AMERICAN HERITAGE CENTER AND ART MUSEUM

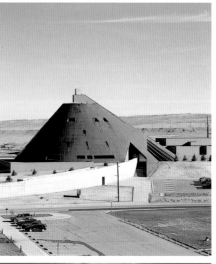

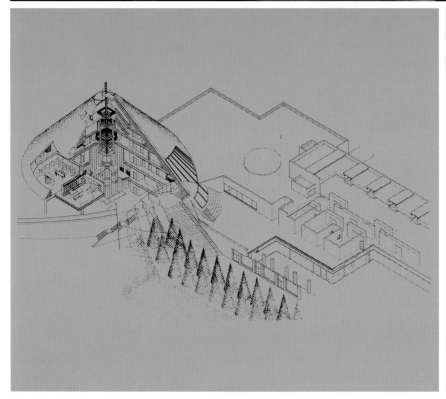

Architect Antoine Predock melded the archetype of the teepee with an interpretation of the mountains and mesas of the American West to create a university museum and heritage center on the edge of the Wyoming campus. The conical shape, in which the archives are found, opens up into a vertiginous form where a wood lattice supports spiraling ramps that rise up around a central hearth. The museum is a village of closed forms at the other end of the mesa. In this project, home on the range is a grand and monumental response to the natural setting.

*clockwise, from top left* view out from the archive building; aerial view; detail of façade; axonometric section | *opposite* archive building

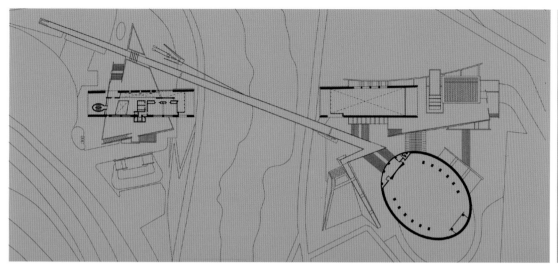

After a new dam had turned part of this secluded valley into a lake, Norihiko Dan designed a community center for the displaced residents. The complex is laid out as a set of fragments on either side of the river, connected by a footbridge. The two main volumes mirror the large wall of the dam upstream and act as a foil to the triangular and oval shapes in front of them. Meeting spaces and a swimming pool offer a habitable continuation of the dam's earthworks.

*opposite, left* aerial view | *opposite, right* aerial view of round bridge | *clockwise, from top left* site plan; view of site; swimming pool; round bridge

# NORIHIKO DAN
# HIYOSHI COMMUNITY CENTER

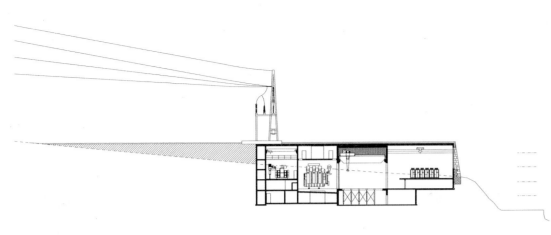

# HANS-JOERG RUCH
# ELECTRICAL SUBSTATION

A piece of engineering is reduced to two visual elements in Albanatscha, Switzerland: a monolithic plinth sliding out of the mountainside, and a mast-like structure that guides the electrical wires into the building. The plinth's chiseled profile provides a contrast to the mountains, incorporating the rugged geology to create a monumental form. The mast and the plinth mark this particular spot in the land where humans have used geography to make power by establishing a place however abstract.

*opposite and left* exterior views showing surrounding mountains I *top left* long section

*above* detail of doorframe

# ANGÉLIL/GRAHAM
# ADIDAS CAMPUS

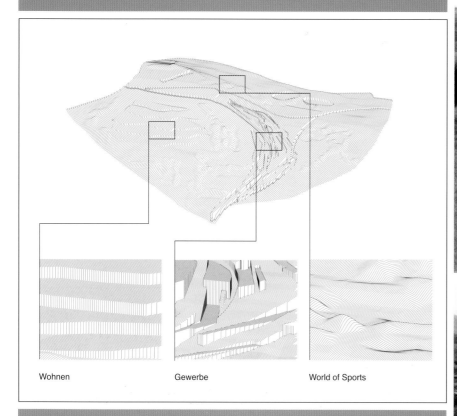

Wohnen          Gewerbe          World of Sports

On the site of a former U.S. army base in Herzogenaurach, Germany, Angélil/Graham has proposed an ambitious combination of housing, shopping, corporate headquarters and brand showcase. The "World of Sports" is a kind of English garden complete with rolling hills and hidden security parameters that separate it from the corporate structures, which, in turn, appear as clumps of trees or hedges. The housing blocks terrace up onto the surrounding hills, increasing the sense that nature is being re-created. The architects use flowing forms and a manipulation of the landscape to suggest the notion of surfing on and through the land.

*above* site plan | *right* views of the complex from the hillside

# 4

# A New Nature
Buildings that merge landscape with architecture, the natural with the human

PETER EISENMAN **WEXNER CENTER**

If it is possible to open up a new nature within the fabric of the land, why not make a totally new nature? Two very different changes in the field of architecture have led practitioners to imagine a landscape whose abstract forms offer new concepts about what it means to build a whole new earth, defying what we consider as base reality. For decades many artists have been trying to come to grips with the most fundamental aspects of our world and then represent them in an alien form. More recently architects have been experimenting with fields of data within computers, which they feel allows them to reconstruct reality.

These "blobmeisters" and other digerati (cyber élite) use computer programs that regard architecture as a body of data that causes a field to assemble itself into forms based on the migration of such information to "attractors," or centers of gravity. These attractors can be natural contours or places of intense use, or they can be idiosyncratic interventions inserted by the programmer or architect. Veering between the desire to create a free and open field and the wish to make wilful form that exhibits itself as a new kind of nature, this latest generation of fieldlike structures reflects the utopian dreams of the earlier proponents of the flat heroic.

The link between the two generations was formed, at least in the U.S., by the work of Peter Eisenman. As a young architect in the early 1960s, he was inspired by the linguistic theories of Noam Chomsky. Eisenman gathered that architecture should be no more and no less than the assembly of a set of signifiers that would, through a contradictory set of relationships established between them, make the user or viewer aware of the inadequacy of any complete and closed linguistic system, including that of architecture. By a continual act of interpretation, viewers would be forced to make sense

of isolated fragments that would seem to frustrate their readings of them—columns hanging in space, lintels on top of nothing, staircases to nowhere.[1]

To avoid these separate pieces coming together into a coherent object sitting in the landscape, Eisenman spent several years pushing and pulling at his house designs until they started to dissolve. Commencing with House X in Michigan (1975), he began to turn his buildings into landscrapers that were partially buried underground, traced the contours of the site, or were the direct translation of his systems of order onto the site. These condensed crystals of the flat heroic suggested that both form and open structure were dead ends. Instead, Eisenman turned object and construction into the act of making an abstract system in and of the land. The logical result would be the disappearance of the maker and the inhabitant in favor of a posthuman structure.[2]

Along with several other architects in the 1980s, Eisenman began to view architecture as a form of mapping. His Romeo & Juliet project of 1985, for instance, proposes architecture as the extrapolation of the multiple interpretations we have laid on the land. The making of things was wrought with problems, Eisenman felt, because it posed an arbitrary object on the land. Instead, architecture should be understood as an exploration—Debord-like—of a terrain, an investigation that transforms it into something we can inhabit first intellectually and later physically. The project consisted of many maps at different scales layered on top of each other and then connected vertically by walls to make spaces. The formal result was an architecture of fragmented extrusion: the transformation of one set of map data into a third dimension, intersected by another set of data that might cut into and deform the first vertical expression.

Eisenman constructed two institutional buildings according to these theories: the Wexner Center for the Visual Arts and Fine Arts Library at Ohio State University in Columbus (1983–89), and the Aronoff Center for Design and Art/DAAP Building at the University of Cincinnati in Ohio (1988–96). The latter, however, showed the mark of Eisenman's new interest—the use of the computer. In computer programs, he had found a form of automatic writing that assembled data into form without human intervention. Forms were inserted ("invaginated," to use the phrase he picked up from Jacques Derrida) into a context that was already seen as the upshot of happenstance. Neither figure nor ground was pure—the computer program alone had logic and consistency.

Eisenman's star pupil of the period, Greg Lynn and his practice FORM took these theories one cogent step further by articulating an architecture of "blobs" and "splines." While the latter were an alternative to central "spines," and represented statistical data that assembled itself along a line of coalescence, the former actually re-proposed form as a new method of coherence. Such form would now be the result of the assembly of energy into a stable configuration. The maximized shape would no longer be restricted by our ability to construct things out of pieces, but could be deposited—much like the geographical process of sedimentation—through the use of computer-aided design, modeling and plastics. Unlike Frank O. Gehry, who uses the same software to create sculptural objects, Lynn sees his work as the intensification and expression of existing conditions into something that is confidently new. His Long Island House (1997) is a "morphing" of site, function and such miscellaneous conditions as a tree, and his proposal for the Port Authority Gateway in New York (1995) turns traffic flows into a snake's pit of undulating forms.[3]

UN STUDIO **ARNHEM STATION**

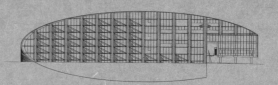

SNØHETTA **BIBLIOTHECA ALEXANDRINA**

A third generation of architects, including Lynn's student Greg Pasquarelli, is now taking these seemingly rigid forms into an altogether more playful direction. With his firm, SHoP (Sharples Holden Pasquarelli), Pasquarelli has designed the Museum of Sex in New York (2001–present), and in the summer of 2000 he produced an installation, Dunescape, at the contemporary art center P.S.1 in Queens, New York (see p. 156). Wood slats curving in several directions at once indicated the underlying, computer-generated order of what was a re-creation of the beach. The planes undulated, giving shelter and soft "dunes" on which visitors could lie. The rigors of a computer-generated form re-created an abstract natural form.

A parallel-running project by the Helsinki office of the multinational firm Foreign Office Architects produced a steel wave that unfolded from one of Helsinki's main streets into a courtyard between two former loading docks. The structure connected the two public spaces and provided a place for performances and leisure activities. As was the case at SHoP's P.S.1, the field of computer-generated pieces reduced itself to not much more than the shaping of a public space. The creation of a defined area of shared and often unscripted activity, though it might seem like an ironic outcome from the semi-scientific research that went into making these structures, is a significant achievement in the commercialized city. It also harks back to the original dreams of joyous exploration that were set forth by such visionaries as Constant Nieuwenhuis.

Dutch architects Ben van Berkel and Caroline Bos work as UN Studio and have long voiced the idea that buildings should be assemblies of data that arise on a site. Yet the practice's constructions have always been translations of the information it has gathered into more or less orthogonal forms. The

architects have proposed a large structure in Arnhem to act as the central transportation hub for this small city. It will not be a structure with a façade, a roof and a ground plane, rather a landscape of continual curves that will dip down for us to walk on it, rise up to shelter us, and open up to allow us to move through it. Within the thickness of its walls myriad programs are accommodated, their existence pushing out the undulating walls of the building into thick nodes of structure and activity. While office buildings will hover above this new landscape, most people will experience the station as a new piece of nature in which movement between different places is celebrated in a space that refuses to remain a static object, and yet has a monumental presence. Its coherence will remind us that it is a human structure whose appearance is due to the interpretation and accumulation of resources in one place, while its convoluted form will erase any sense of articulation that specifies this fact.[4]

Is this the future of the flat heroic: giant structures that float in and out of the ground, remaining open to interpretation and use, and referring to themselves as products of a new nature? If they are not the harbingers of a future family of forms, they will certainly contribute to a type of architecture in which the edges of form are continually being elided by the electronic movement of information and the restless toing and froing of people and goods. The emergence of a service-based economy has done away with many stand-alone factories and housing blocks, replacing them with massive "attractors," such as airports, shopping malls, trans-shipment centers or distribution centers and sports stadia, all of which hug the land and many of which coalesce into complete cities. Computers continue to minimize the space we need for physical objects while we demand increasing freedom of movement. Perhaps we will soon see the disappearance

of the distinct art of architecture and even of the coherent city in favor of a new landscape of dispersion. There the only signs of human society will be fluid, open-ended structures that rise naturally from the land. These structures will be the result of the assembly of data into centers where we will come together to enjoy, explore and investigate our world in an almost ritualistic manner.[5]

A prototype, where form does not directly mimic the flow of data as it appears on a computer screen, might be the Bibliotheca Alexandrina in Egypt (1990–2001, see p. 168). Designed by the Oslo-based firm Snøhetta (Craig Dykers, Christoph Kapeller and Kjetil T. Thorsen), it is a structure that seeks to rebuild the fabled library, once the center of classical civilization, but is not the result of the need to house a collection of any size. Its impetus is symbolic, hoping to serve as an attractor that will generate visits to and interest in this Third World city. Floating at the edge of the harbor, it presents only a semicircular grid to the outside world. Appearing to be the leftover scaffolding from some fragmentary pyramid, the library proclaims the unfinished nature of construction. Inside, a vast reading room spreads out underneath a coffered ceiling.

The most obvious model for the Bibliotheca Alexandrina is the Tower of Babel, and this might be the archetype of the flat heroic. In these forms, we build a new nature that accommodates the richness of our experiences and needs, while remaining stable and coherent enough to establish a communal place. The Tower of Babel will never be a landscraper, but the desire to build such structures will remain and will translate into forms that will scrape the land, transforming it, hollowing it out, lifting it up, remaking and remolding it, but never escaping from the earthbound reality.

DAN KILEY **MILLER GARDEN**

MICHAEL HEIZER **CITY**

If we are to have a world not just filled with such Babylonian structures, which are expensive, but rather one that is turned into landscapes that are the result of the condensation of data into public buildings, the question would be: what do they look like, what governs their design? The traditions of architecture would barely seem adequate at this scale, intensity and semi-automatic agglomeration of data. In fact, some of the behemoths now appearing out of computers and onto the landscape suffer from bland monotony that arises from the utter lack of control certain architects have over their new materials. We must all turn to the traditions of shaping the land and the art forms that have come out of the venerable history of landscape architecture.

Garden design has long offered a "second nature." Human intervention in the garden has almost always produced an artificial environment in spite of the garden's raw materials—plants, flowers, trees and grasses. While Roman gardens were filled with tricks and focused on colonnades and other building fragments, medieval gardens were laid out in geometric patterns with their boundaries, even in the *hortus conclusus* or secret garden, remaining simple walls. In the Renaissance, walls disappeared completely from sight; only the geometry of plantings was left. Essentially, these types of garden design were a pure manipulation of the land and what grows on it.[6]

The Baroque garden began to break the rigidity of the garden plan into isolated episodes, overlapping layers of planting, interwoven sequences and other complex forms that made the designer's imposition on the land more and more invisible. Following Lancelot "Capability" Brown (1716–83) and the emergence of the so-called English Garden with its flowing contours that sought to perfect nature into picturesque compositions instead of imposing pre-ordained paths on the

earth, such counterfeit reached new heights of sophistication. With hidden ditches that kept sheep off the lawn, trees planted to look as if they had grouped themselves in an attractive composition, and the land shaped as if following the waves of pleasantly undulating geology, the English Garden presented a full picture of "nature."[7]

By the advent of the modernist aesthetic, which sought to depict the technological character of a continually changing world, landscape design had become a problematic pursuit. Few designers genuinely tried to express nature, and some felt as if their profession should disappear, as the design of individual buildings might, into the act of planning. Landscapes should guide cars, watercourses or other means of movement through the land. They should make the technology of agriculture visible, or define the voids that were the counterpoint to the abstract building blocks decreed by architects.[8] Only a handful of designers, such as Dan Kiley in the u.s., offered an alternative vision of landscape design as something that would continue the lines of dissolution promulgated by modernist architecture into the surroundings while catching small moments of rest, order and difference between such vectors.

In other words, designers began to make spaces and forms from nature that did not try to look like plants or buildings, but that were hybrid abstractions of both. The designer was granted a free gesture: a fountain of great swirling power, a moment of pure color or a swerving line that led nowhere. Landscape design made its own place. In the Miller Garden by Dan Kiley in Columbus, Indiana (1955), the effect was truly liberating. Free from the constraints of habitation and the vagaries of untrained planting materials, this ordered environment offered an alternative to culture and nature.[9]

There is a direct relationship between this form of landscape architecture and what critic Rosalind Krauss called "sculpture in the expanded field."[10] At the intersection of figuration, abstraction, planning and gesture, she posits, the making of a particular form in a certain place for a moment in time occurs. Site-specific work means to reveal the nature of its location in time and space, the history of its making, the hand of its maker, and the cultural assumptions that maker and viewer bring to an experience of the work. The result is something that is neither object nor field. The work creates an environment, but is also an object (or set of objects) in its own right. It offers an alternative landscape that is critical of, or merely makes us aware of, what we have left behind once we are in a position to experience the site-specific piece.[11]

Some artists aim to produce complex and highly distinct versions of such work, but it is at its most effective when it is executed at a vast scale that permits the artist to control our experience. Earth art, as it is called, was pioneered by such artists as Robert Smithson. His "spiral jetties" in Utah (1970) and the Netherlands (1971) are giant, abstract forms that can only be experienced fully from the air. They are paths that slowly remove the user from the land, surrounding her or him with the void of water, and then turn further and further in on themselves, so that the user finally becomes lost at the spiral's center. A new world is evoked, made as a piece of sculpture, but existing as an almost pure manipulation of space.[12]

Michael Heizer has engaged in the long and patient construction of a separate family of forms. After such initial gestures of cutting into the land as Double Negative (1969–70), a v-shaped incision in a cliff north of Las Vegas, Heizer retreated to a remote and secret desert valley in New Mexico

DONALD JUDD **THE CHINATI FOUNDATION**

ALLIED WORKS ARCHITECTURE **MARYHILL NATURE OVERLOOK**

to build City (1972–76). This seems to be—he does not allow visitors yet—a counterproposal to the landscape of the American Southwest. Its mastaba-like appearance reflects the buttes and mesas around the site, while its L-shaped forms resemble ruins of a former civilization or the building blocks for a new one. This is a city of forms rather than one of habitation: the essence of human construction standing on one of the most essentially abstract landscapes Heizer could find.[13]

In a similar setting, James Turrell has been working underground. Since 1972, he has been digging tunnels and chambers into the remains of Roden Crater, an extinct volcano. The axes these cuts delineate line up with astral and sidereal activity, enabling viewers to align themselves with the movement of the planets, including the earth. "Skyspaces" make visitors aware of the exact quality of light and the shape of the sky. Other spaces and lines reveal the curvature of the earth. By removing everything else, Turrell wants us to come to a full understanding of where we are. This project is one of the purest revelations of time and space ever attempted, and it promises to make a landscape at such a vast and otherwise undefinable scale that the true act of experiencing the earth will be liberated within its confines.[14]

Artists have tried in the past to integrate abstract landscapes into the traditions of place making. While Walter de Maria's Lightning Field of 1977 reveals bolts of lightning as they come down into the New Mexico Plains, it is also a field of metal rods that makes visible the agricultural and planning grids Americans have laid over the whole continent. It is a line of telephone poles that has become a grid, an abstract field of measurement that shows how we seek to control nature.[15] For The Chinati Foundation (1979–86) in Marfa, Texas, Donald Judd (1928–94) stripped former army barracks of as much definition as possible so that they now not only house his

abstract sculptures, but also begin to approach his pieces in their expression of geometric solids. There is an emptiness in such spaces that makes one concentrate on pure form and pure void.[16]

When the architect and artist Lauretta Vinciarelli was residing in Marfa and helping to draw up plans for the renovation, she began to draw the spaces. As she drew, her images became more and more fanciful. At first they depicted the buildings and surrounding landscape, but they soon became rooms filled with water, shot through with light and disappearing into unfathomable distances. Light, form, color, and shade shaped compositions that resembled a form of architecture removed from use. One could imagine inhabiting the spaces in her watercolors, but only as a mental act. What mattered was her study of how light shapes form, how color models solids, and how space emerges from these phenomena. There is no scale to such landscapes, and no direction. They are abstract, other worlds.

In more recent drawings, Vinciarelli has removed even the land. In its place she gives us a plane that could be water or sky, in which objects float. These "wings" mimic the movement of a swimmer's arms through a pool, or a jet fighter's wings through air, fixing movement as a hovering solid. In other drawings only the frame remains in front of a gradation of color that implies a landscape, but never allows it to become recognizable. Vinciarelli's architecture disappears almost entirely into the act of representation we would class as painting.[17]

Certainly paintings propose other lands that we could inhabit, from the realistically rendered fantasy of seventeenth-century French painter Claude Lorrain (1600–82) to the hovering solids of Mark Rothko (1903–70). Yet these spaces are resolutely unreal. The impulse behind them is to offer

something that is completely other. Such art removes itself from our daily experience. This is also true of site-specific sculpture, even when it exists as public artworks in a city center. It always comments on, or offers an alternative to, the spaces we inhabit every day. Architects and landscape architects learn from this kind of art. If they sometimes hover, as Vinciarelli does, on the edge of having their proposals for construction fade into fantastic and dissolving form, at other times they attempt to integrate objects and spaces of pure experience into built form.

One of the most successful examples of such an attempt is Oregon practice Brad Cloepfil/Allied Works Architecture's Maryhill Nature Overlook on the edge of the Columbia River Gorge (see p. 162). Designed as a visitor center on the estate of entrepreneur Samuel Hill, the concrete ribbon that unfolds along the cliff's edge is part of a series of investigations into man-made and natural edges in which Cloepfil has been engaged for the last decade.

Making a new landscape as a constructed environment is informing, if not always dominating, the work of many of the world's best architects, and their working methods further develop the notion of landscapers. In many of Antoine Predock's designs, for instance, buildings become man-made mesas through which he carves winding passages. The interiors are fairly standard rooms, but the visitor must undertake a journey of discovery through an artificial landscape shaped by concrete, glass and strong planes of light penetrating into the building's depth to find these spaces. In the administration building for the University of California at Pomona (1993), a portion of the roof is occupiable. It is an outdoor amphitheater where one can watch the planes as they line up to land at Los Angeles International Airport fifty miles away. The building becomes a solid object to be

STEVEN HOLL **PROJECT FOR PHOENIX**

KOLATAN/MAC DONALD STUDIO **RESI/RISE**

explored, and its roof becomes a place from which one can admire the human and the natural lines that shape our experience of space.

Steven Holl, an architect working in New York, has provided a theoretical base for these design practices. In his 1981 essay "Parallax View" (written to explain his competition design for Porta Vittoria, Milan), Holl argued that the act of building could be reduced to a phenomenal understanding of whether one was on, below or above the earth. By weaving together experiences of the land, the architect could create an organic sequence of spaces that would develop their own narrative of occupation.[18] He elaborated on these proposals in *Edge of a City*, a book that presents five interconnected designs he produced between 1989 and 1999 for six cities in the U.S. (see p. 172). The most striking was a line of buildings for Phoenix, Arizona's northern boundary. Intended as a type of dam against sprawl, this wall of lofts falls apart into horizontal and vertical tubes, recalling Sol LeWitt's experiments in the different permutations of an open cube during the 1960s and 1970s. Functioning as geometry and urbanism at a vast scale, the open web of construction offers a human alternative to the surrounding mountains and desert, combining their lines with the insides and infrastructure of the confused world of suburban development to create a clear and visible monument.[19]

Several buildings designed by Basel-based firm Herzog & de Meuron respond to nature not by deferring to it but by establishing new spaces and forms from which it can be understood. The architects often camouflage the buildings' skins so that they can fit into either urban or natural sites. For example, in the 1998 Sports Hall outside Basel, they used a photographic etching technique to give the building a leaflike texture, and in a small artist's studio (1998), they encouraged

mold to grow on the concrete façade. The architects employ these techniques to express the buildings' elemental geometry more strongly. Instead of associating the forms with a particular material, or seeing the building as a monumental object, we begin to appreciate it as a condensation, combination and transformation of program and site into a unified entity.

Their most successful response to the landscape is evident in the Dominus Winery in Napa Valley, California (1996–98, see p. 158): a simple block placed on a lightly sloping vineyard. The structure stands against the backdrop of hills, making a line that helps us understand the gentle slope of the land toward them. Herzog & de Meuron constructed the winery from local rocks contained within the gabions that usually hold back rocks in road cuts. The building thus takes the land, shapes it into a simple form we can understand, and then aids our comprehension of the lie of the land. Inside this landscape gesture hover open glass offices and closed industrial sheds. Visitors look through the rocks of this man-made cave to the tasting room, a windowless and ceremonial room in which they can see the grapes gathered from the surrounding vineyard turn into wine. Culture and cultivation come together in this singular object.

The relationship between culture and cultivation is at the heart of French practice François et Associés. Some of the architects' larger designs call for the mimicking of nature through built form, while others seem to elaborate on what is already on the landscape and what humans have done to nature. In their 1996 project for a technical school in Savigny-sur-Orge, France, they unearthed the watercourse used to feed the moat of the castle on whose grounds they were building, and then broke their buildings into parallel blocks with open views of the tree branches. Their most successful design, however, is for ten vacation homes in Jupilles, France (1996,

see p. 174). Taking the implication of Sea Ranch one step further, they turned the homes into hedgerows, letting vegetation grow on screens to form façades. Architecture dissolves into a texture that melds with nature. It is not an original and untroubled natural condition that François et Associés is resurrecting, but a new and wholly artificial environment that marries landscaping and building traditions into coherent form.

These types of buildings share a sculptural sense of making form out of materials that are as massive or as simple as the natural conditions in which they are sited. Other architects, however, attempt to turn the urban landscape into similarly strong forms. In 1978, Dutch architect Rem Koolhaas wrote a book proposing a set of landscrapers for Manhattan that would create the imaginary and imaginative heart of a reborn metropolis. A swimming pool swum by the force of the swimmers themselves from Russia to New York, The Hotel Sphinx, "City of the Captive Globe" and "New Welfare Island" were all condensations of the grids, spires, cubes, and internal realms of fantasy Koolhaas believed gave force to what he called "Manhattanism." Within their highly collaged forms, fragments of the city became three-dimensional objects that could be seen from all sides. Koolhaas extracted the essence of architecture from its most developed form—the large city—and condensed it into something that resembled a stratified rock or a geode. A new nature was boiled down to the point where it was something the architect could carve, build on, or merely reveal.[20]

Koolhaas's vision has been developed by the firm Kolatan/Mac Donald. In their Rooftop Garden (1996) and Resi/Rise (1999) projects, the architects use computers to present a fluid landscape that cuts through the Manhattan skyline. In the earlier project, they re-use and connect midtown

REM KOOLHAAS **ROTTERDAM KUNSTHAL**

VICENTE GUALLART **ARTIFICIAL LANDSCAPE**

WEST 8 **SCHOUWBURGPLEIN**

rooftops into a landscape of fluid forms. Nature regained for human occupation buries or camouflages territorial and constructional differences underneath an Edenic vision and also liberates the fluidity that buildings had replaced. In Resi/Rise, the landscape condenses into high-rise flats that are clad in bulbous shapes. They seem to bulge out from the high-rise while maintaining a sense of the overall order of the skyscraper that is not one of the relation of parts, but of the overall build-up of related forms. The building is nature made into a solid object for human occupation.

Meanwhile, Koolhaas has tried to put into practice his semi-utopian visions of the city—as an organic landscape built up out of the complexity of its own construction—by designing structures he believes translate the essence of urbanity into built form. As his architecture has progressed, he has replaced the monolithic tendencies of his earlier buildings with highly intricate open volumes that push and pull through each other. In the Rotterdam Kunsthal of 1990, for instance, the walkway connecting a low-lying park with the level of the dyke on which the building is located rises up gradually, broadening along the way into a sloping auditorium. A second walkway leads up from the top of the auditorium to a bridge over the first walkway before terminating at an inclined and planted plane on the exterior, pointing up to the sky. Through and between the planes, the volumes for the art display open up. Various structural systems, including metal pipes and what appear to be tree trunks (which actually contain steel columns) hold together the spaces. What is ground and what is ceiling, what is man-made and what is natural, what is void and what is solid are not so much confused as they keep changing into each other through the peculiar alchemy of the architecture. Koolhaas does not make buildings in the landscape—with façades, floor plans and suites of rooms—he makes buildings

as landscapes in which the land becomes a building face and the interior is only a seamless convolution of the exterior's order into labyrinthine caves.

Koolhaas continues to develop more complex combinations of forms and planes, spiraling them up into fantastic layer-cake structures like the Seattle Public Library, but several of his former employees have managed to discipline and abstract the technique even further. Koolhaas's influence can be seen in such places as Slovenia, where the firm Njiric & Njiric, based in Zagreb, Croatia, has designed a shopping mall with parking levels and billboards that are composed of interpenetrating horizontal and vertical forms, which then flesh out into the actual programmatic spaces.

In Thom Henrehan's project for Tokyo Bay (2000) a whole city emerges out of the water's edge. The freeways and containers of goods and people merge to become an integrated structure whose roof is free for play. Building on the architect's earlier experiments with the making of landscrapers that drove into and opened up the earth, this theoretical design takes his ideas to a much larger and syncretic level. Tokyo Bay is a proposal for a new city with a clear form that also re-weaves Tokyo's infrastructure.

ACTAR Arquitectura[21] (a loose grouping of theorists, writers and designers) in Barcelona and architect Vicente Guallart have created artificial landscapes by making a collage of landscape forms on the computer. Working with advertising imagery but respectful of the undulations of the existing landscape, the Barcelona architects seem most interested in combining an archaeology of consumer culture with an investigation of physical landforms to create an artificial nature. Harking back to the fantasies of Constant and the slick, filmic visions of Koolhaas, their work is part commentary

part proposal for a world in which technology has freed us to find our own little plot of nature however manufactured.

Dutch firm West 8 has constructed fragments of artificiality within the urban grid. Basing their work on drawings similar to those produced by Marianne Vriesendorp for Koolhaas, the architects developed the Schouwburgplein project in a Rotterdam square (1991–97), which makes the presence of a parking lot an excuse for creating a plinth of wood and monumental exhaust vents on its roof. The firm activates these urban activities with a line of spotlights that each visitor can use to highlight some fragment or occurrence on this urban stage. In the project, architecture is a ground condition that unfolds into a collection of open planes and machines that are necessary and playful.

MVRDV has designed some of the most fantastically complex landscrapers. The Villa VPRO (1997) is the headquarters of a broadcasting company, where the design begins in the parking lots. Cars park in front of and underneath the building. The pavement then continues in through the reception area and up into the office areas as a steep flow of concrete along which emblems of domesticity, such as a Persian carpet and a formal chair, lie scattered. The office floors spiral up in a pattern that does not distinguish between specific levels, but differentiates the working areas.

A steep canyon cuts into the building's heart, while some of the steps make informal auditoria, which the building steps up through a tiered cafeteria and out onto the roof terrace. The terrace is not a plane of stone or concrete, but an undulating grass field that brings the interior steps back to a natural condition. The Villa VPRO is a building without base or roof and without very clearly articulated façades. Instead it is a machine for processing, subdividing and re-ordering the landscape that results in an idyllic vision of nature regained.

MVRDV **VILLA VPRO**

MVRDV employed this bucolic vision in their design for the Dutch pavilion at the Hanover World's Fair of 2000 (see p. 150). The architects created fragments of the Dutch landscape on each floor of the building: a carpet of flower bulbs, water that courses through so much of the land, and the intense urban conglomerations. These elements are not contained within a single shape, but exist as autonomous worlds stacked on top of each other. At the pavilion's top they placed a grid of windmills to power the whole structure. MVRDV lifted technology and nature up to a plane of perfection, way above the ground plane's more confusing reality.

These artificial and condensed landscrapers promise to give us back the land and architecture. By making us aware of the simple facts of the ground we inhabit, we can regain a sense of the reality of place in a culture that is more and more dependent on the abstraction engendered by instant communication, digital manipulation and the mass production of real and virtual spaces. By proposing to turn objects and fields—the most elemental making of territory, which we know as landscape architecture—into forms that respond to our body and our landscape, the architects make concrete the realities of human culture. In so doing, landscrapers might be the building blocks for an architecture refound and given a new foundation in the land.

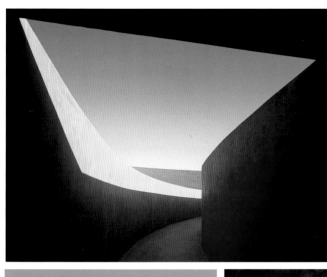

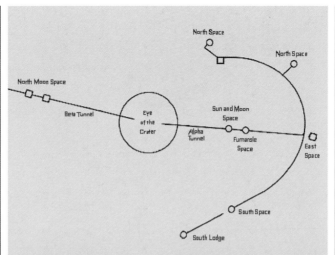

# JAMES TURRELL
# RODEN CRATER

To make us aware of the most ephemeral and yet most fundamental realities of the physical world, artist James Turrell has spent the last quarter of a century shaping the remains of a volcano into a giant observatory in the Arizona desert. "Sky spaces" make the visitor aware of the weight and shape of the heavens, a 1000-foot-long (305 meters) tunnel frames for an instant the moon at its end and a path lets the visitor experience the curvature of the earth. Here, the earth is formed, abstracted and revealed in its essence.

*opposite* view of crater from desert | *clockwise, from top left* entrance pathway; schematic site plan; tunnel *overleaf* interior and exterior view of "sky spaces"

A layercake of synthetic landscapes, the pavilion at the Hanover Expo exhibited the notion that the Dutch live in an artificial landscape. Visitors rose up past planted forests and fields of tulips, interrupted by the type of insistent construction that permeates the Dutch landscape and breaks it into alternating fragments of urban and agricultural scenes. They finally reached a viewing deck where a grid of high-tech windmills offered a twenty-first-century antidote to the country's traditional image.

*opposite* ground level I *left* exterior view I *below, top* circulation space I *below, bottom* viewing deck

# MVRDV
# **DUTCH PAVILION**

This combination of a tram terminal, maintenance facility and park-and-ride garage nestles between a highway, with its on- and off-ramps, and housing blocks. The structure's curved spaces are composed from what is left over after the tram has arrived and been served and the cars have been parked. By bringing light deep into the sloped site in Nice, France, local architect Marc Barani has made the station areas habitable while emphasizing the movement of all the different traffic systems over and under each other.

*far left* site plan | *left* aerial view | *below* tramlines | *opposite, top* view of roof

*opposite, bottom* terminal in its urban context

# MARC BARANI
# NICE TRAMWAY TERMINAL

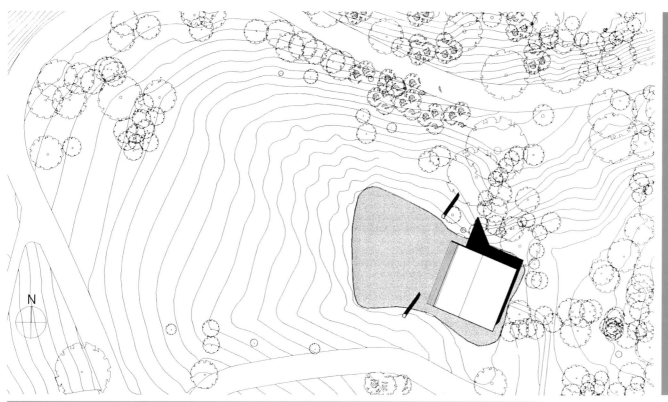

*left* site plan | *below, top* cross section | *below, bottom* plan | *opposite, clockwise from top* view from rear; distance view; view from pool

# IAN RITCHIE ARCHITECTS
## CRYSTAL PALACE
## CONCERT PLATFORM

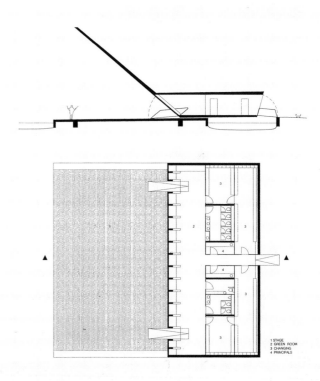

1 STAGE
2 GREEN ROOM
3 CHANGING
4 PRINCIPALS

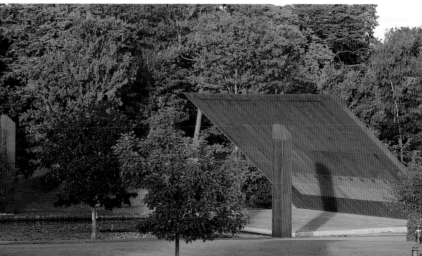

# SHoP
# DUNESCAPE

In the summer of 2000, a beach appeared in the middle of Queens, New York. As part of an ongoing series of site-specific installations by architects at P.S.1 Contemporary Art Center, New York collaborative SHoP used closely spaced slats to lay out a rippling landscape through the courtyards in front of the building. Lawn chairs and beach umbrellas completed the feel of sandy beaches and dunes frozen into hillocks and caves, but whose articulate surfaces gave them an urban sensibility. In May 1968, the situationists promised "the beach below the paving stones." SHoP, however, made a new beach—perhaps revolution can be avoided through art?

*opposite* view toward P.S.1 I *left* the installation was comprised of cedar slats I *below* digital rendering

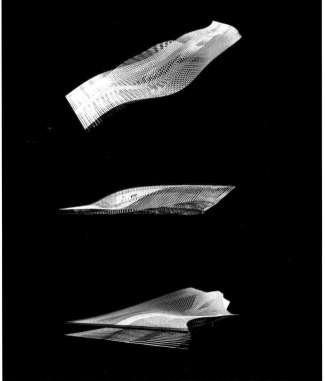

In the 50,000-square-foot (4645-square-meter) winery in Yountville, CA, Herzog and de Meuron have turned parallel lines of vines into a built mass that runs alongside and mimics the hills behind it. The architects used gabions filled with local stones to create a sheltering volume. The actual offices and production spaces sit in glass and concrete volumes inside this shell.

*left* natural light penetrates the interior | *below left* the gabions are filled with local basalt | *opposite* view from vineyard

# HERZOG & DE MEURON
## DOMINUS WINERY

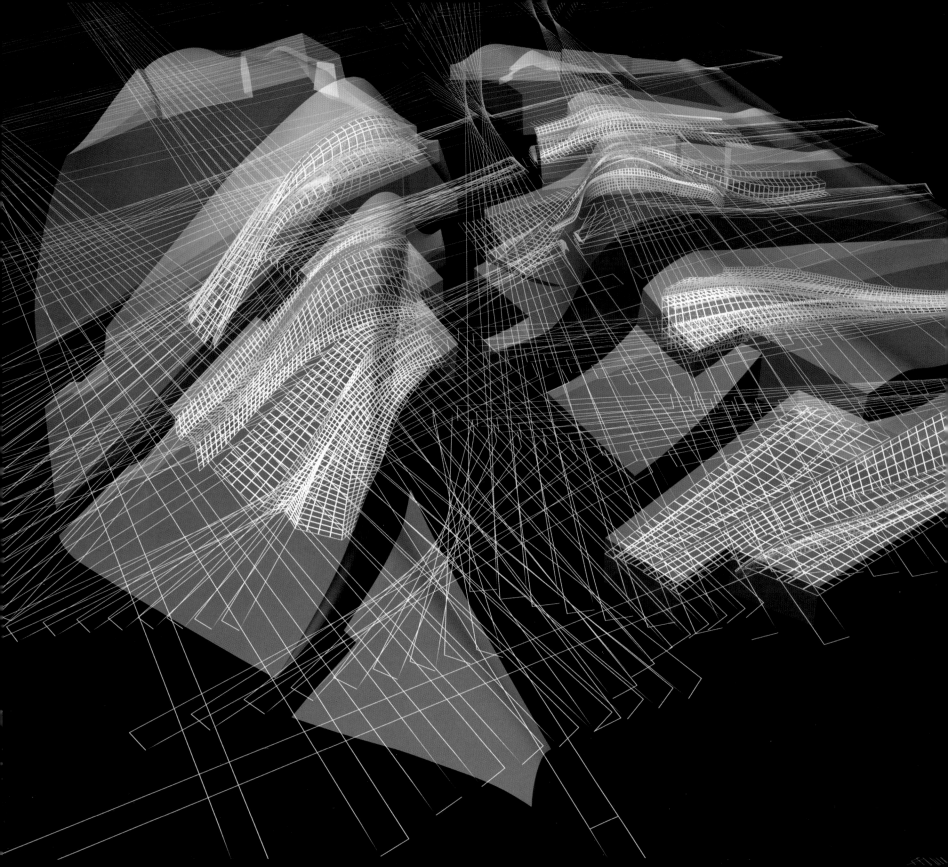

The design for a large complex of cultural facilities in Santiago de Compostela was produced by overlaying a warped version of the streets of this ancient Spanish pilgrimage town with an orthogonal grid. The complex was then covered with an undulating shroud, bringing a sense of mystery and the unknown to the expository and investigatory functions of the library, museum and opera house below. Inside, the relationship between the structuring systems was manipulated to accentuate the differences between our various interpretations of man's ability to order nature.

# PETER EISENMAN
# CITY OF CULTURE

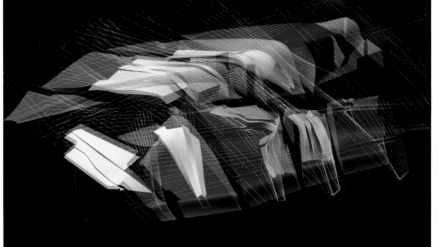

*opposite and left* digital renderings | *top* model

# ALLIED WORKS ARCHITECTURE
## MARYHILL NATURE OVERLOOK

Brad Cloepfil, principal of Allied Works Architecture, bases many of his projects on the investigation into man-made and natural edges, involving the lines we use as paths through the landscape. At the overlook on the edge of the Columbia River Gorge, the line lifts up to become a portal, dives into the ground to provide seating, and always points toward the endless vista across the gorge. It makes a place in a vast plain, yet does not enclose anything. It is only the merest hint of the difference that architecture can make in and on the land.

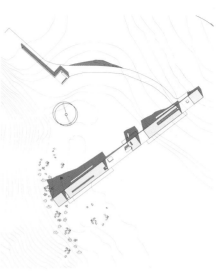

*right* site plan | *below top* the overlook is 150 feet in length | *below bottom and opposite* the single concrete band points out over the gorge

Making a new ground in a bit of sprawl that has spread to the far reaches of central Europe, this Croatian firm treated the irregular site as a single volume into which a series of rectangular bays was cut. The garden and home improvement center in Maribor, Slovenia has glazed surfaces only toward these courtyards. The roof is open and publicly accessible. The hypermarket becomes a new terrain organized around billboards that turn out to be the center's only clear identity.

*opposite* **visitors can access the turfed roof |** *clockwise,* *from top left* **the urban context; model; an opaque façade faces the road; the billboard stands out from its surroundings; long section**

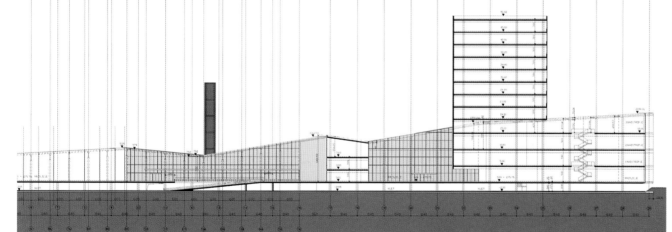

# NJIRIC & NJIRIC
# BAUMAXX HYPERMARKET

There are few more ambitious counterfeits of nature than Barcelona-based Vicente Guallart's project in Denia, an ancient coastal town in the east of Spain. Guallart, who has long been interested in architecture as a form of artificial landscape, used computer programs to generate a geometric mound. His aim was to reconstruct a modern version of the castle-topped mountain, inside which would be a cultural center, commercial facilities and a hotel.

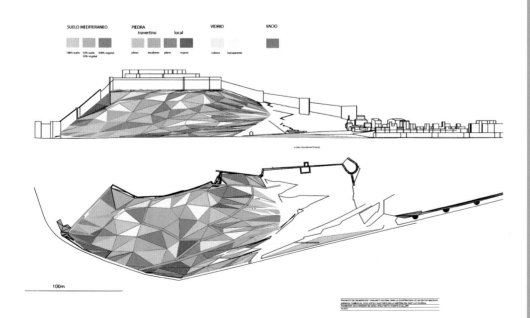

SUELO MEDITERANEO    PIEDRA    VIDRIO    VACIO

100m

**opposite** site view with [bottom] and without [top] the cultural park in place I **above** view from street I **left** elevation [top], plan [bottom]

BIBLIOTHECA ALEXANDRINA
NORTH EAST ELEVATION

10    20    30    40    50

# SNØHETTA
# BIBLIOTHECA ALEXANDRINA

In an attempt to recapture the glories of ancient days, the Egyptian government commissioned an international competition for a new library in Alexandria. It was won by an Oslo-based group of young architects with a scheme for a giant, terraced circular space set into and rising out of its waterfront site. The exterior is covered with calligraphic letters and inscriptions from civilizations around the world. The building as a whole recalls ancient hypostyle halls and earthworklike burial monuments.

*opposite* view toward waterfront I *top* north-east elevation I *bottom* the monumental form sits easily in its surroundings I *overleaf* a bridge connects the nearby university to the library I *p. 171, clockwise, from left* letters and inscriptions cover the exterior; night view; interior space

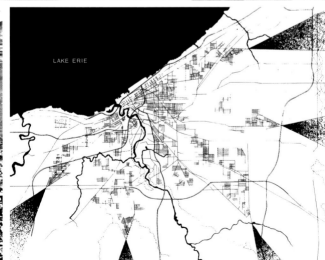

# STEVEN HOLL
## EDGE OF A CITY

LAKE ERIE

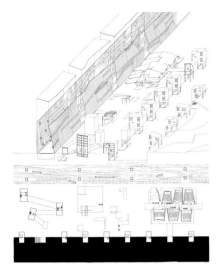

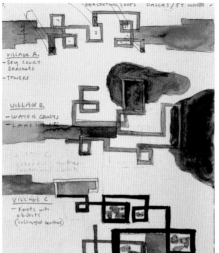

As part of his ongoing investigations into the formal properties of architecture, Steven Holl embarked on a series of projects that would collect, frame and order the sprawling metropolis in the U.S. L-shaped towers would form an edge against the desert in Phoenix, AZ; a knot of different functions would stand amid the freeway interchanges of Dallas and Fort Worth, TX; an x-shaped building would become the focal point for the suburbs of Cleveland, OH; artists' housing would bring craftsmanship back to the Erie Canal in upstate New York. Each of these projects treated urban forces as the constituents for giant sculptures that would respond to the natural settings with human objects of an equal scale and force.

*opposite, clockwise from top* sketch of housing at Erie Canal; site plan of Cleveland; aerial view of Phoenix
*clockwise, from top left* elevation of housing at Erie Canal; sketch of buildings at Dallas and Fort Worth; model of building at Dallas and Fort Worth; aerial view of x-shaped building at Cleveland

# FRANÇOIS ET ASSOCIÉS
## RURAL HOLIDAY HOUSES

Instead of making holiday homes that recall "rural traditions" or "local vernacular," François et Associés decided to hide these occasional retreats for urbanites in hedgerows. The rows of houses in Jupilles, France are situated in wild and unkempt grass and surrounded by forest. Each dwelling is a simple, elongated box composed of glass and wood, with outdoor storage. The vegetation is trained to cover the homes' shapes so that they are clearly volumes of habitation, but also building blocks for a new kind of artificial nature.

*above, from top* south elevation; terrace, ground-level and first-level plans; cross sections
*top right* the homes are situated on the forest edge | *right* interior spaces are very simple
*opposite* vegetation disguises the houses' shape

# References

### INTRODUCTION

**1** The canonical text for reviewing the definitions of architecture as a primarily notional shelter is Joseph Rykwert's *On Adam's House in Paradise: The Idea of the Primitive Hut in Architectural History* (Cambridge, MA: The MIT Press, 2nd ed., 1981). At the heart of Rykwert's argument is the notion of the "aedicula," the most elemental device for defining place as explained by Sir John Summerson in his essay "Heavenly Mansions" in his *Heavenly Mansions and Other Essays on Architecture* (New York, NY: W W Norton & Company, 1963): 1–28. Such discourses are biased toward construction as an artificial ordering system and oppose the more mystical and vague tradition explored by Christian Norberg-Schulz in *Intentions in Architecture* (Cambridge, MA: The MIT Press, 1966) and in *The Concept of Dwelling: On the Way to a Figurative Architecture* (New York, NY: Rizzoli International Publications, 1985) and by Gaston Bachelard in *The Poetics of Space*, trans. Maria Jolas (Boston, MA: Beacon Press, 1964).

**2** Vitruvius, *De Architectura. The Ten Books on Architecture*, trans. Morris Hicky Morgan (New York, NY: Dover Publications, 1967).

**3** Architecture lost its direct connection to the military and defense when the Ecole des Beaux-Arts was set up in 1648. It would be interesting to trace the remnants of military imagery in the architecture of the nineteenth and twentieth centuries, which, to my knowledge, has never been done. It is worth noting that much of the civic and cultural space in the European cities of today was constructed in the land opened up by the tearing down of fortifications that started in the mid-nineteenth century. Thus, the landscape that constitutes much of the visible and experiential elements of what we consider as urbanity was defined by the necessities of war. Similarly, Baron Hausmann introduced the "grands boulevards" in Paris in the 1860s, which serve not only for civic beautification and efficiency, but also to control crowds. Finally, the language of war was translated into the war on disease and poverty that was used to justify much of modern architecture and urban planning. See Anthony Vidler, *The Writing of the Walls: Architectural Theory in the Late Enlightenment* (New York, NY: Princeton Architectural Press, 1989). For a discussion on the contemporary complicity of architecture and war see Manuel DeLanda, *War in the Age of Intelligent Machines* (New York, NY: Zone Books, 1992), and Nan Ellin, ed., *Architecture of Fear* (New York, NY: Princeton Architectural Press, 1997).

**4** See Vincent Scully, *The Earth, the Temple and the Gods: Greek Sacred Architecture* (New Haven, CT: Yale University Press, rev. ed., 1980). Scully's early work established the basis for much of his (and, as one of his many thousands of students, my) thinking about the relationship between building and land. Late in his life, Scully came back to some of these themes in *Architecture: The Natural and the Manmade* (New York, NY: St. Martin's Press, 1991).

**5** Anthony Vidler, *The Architectural Uncanny: Essays in the Modern Unhomely* (Cambridge, MA: The MIT Press, 1992).

**6** Lucius Annaeus Seneca, *Letters from a Stoic*, trans. Robin Campbell (New York, NY: Penguin Books, 1969). The interest in the healing qualities of the land has a long cultural history. For a full review of the literary side of this fascination see E. Kegel Brinkgreve's *The Echoing Woods: Bucolic and Pastoral from Theocritus to Wordsworth* (Amsterdam: J. C. Gieben, 1990). The most popular text on the topic remains Simon Schama, *Landscape and Memory* (London: Fontana Press, 1996). For a treatment of the cultural and aesthetic conditions of the landscape see Elizabeth Barlow Rogers, *Landscape Design: A Cultural and Architectural History* (New York, NY: Stewart, Tabori & Chang, 2001).

**7** In a project by conceptual artists Vitaly Komar and Alex Melamid, an international audience was asked what their ideal picture was. In almost all cases it was a natural scene with animals, water and woods. Joann Wypijewski, ed., *Painting by Numbers: Komar & Melamid's Scientific Guide to Art* (Berkeley, CA: University of California Press, 1999).

**8** For two books on the subject see David Pearson, *New Organic Architecture: the Breaking Wave* (Berkeley, CA: University of California Press, 2001) and Eugene Tsui, *Evolutionary Architecture: Nature as a Basis for Design* (New York, NY: John Wiley & Sons, 1999).

**9** Germany led the trend with its *Gesetz zur Einsparung von Energie in Gebäuden* (energy-conservation law in buildings), promulgated on 22 July 1976. Most other Northern European countries followed suit and tightened standards. In 1993, the German government published an adapted building code that specified, for example, the distance to an outside window in an office building. Again, this law was adopted in other countries and will probably become part of European Community standards.

**10** This tendency is discussed in Aaron Betsky, *Building Sex: Men, Women, Architecture and the Construction of Sexuality* (New York, NY: William Morrow, 1995). See also Mario Praz, *An Illustrated History of Interior Decoration: From Pompeii to Art Nouveau* (London: Thames & Hudson, 1982).

**11** The relationship between geologic and human time was made explicit by John A. McPhee in his essays and books that he drew together as *Annals of the Former World* (New York, NY: Farrar, Straus & Giroux, 1998), and in *Assembling California* (New York, NY: Farrar, Straus & Giroux, 1993). It was also the basis for much of the thinking in the work of John Brincherhoff Jackson, especially the essays collected in his *A Sense of Place, a Sense of Time* (New Haven, CT: Yale University Press, 1994). The connection was drawn by William Rees Morrish, ed., in his series *Civilizing Terrains – Mountains, Mounds and Mesas* (London: Art Data, 1996).

**12** He discussed this topic during his lectures and to my knowledge no documentation exists.

**13** This is evident in the rise of such organizations as the Alliance for Historic Landscape Preservation in the United States. The National Trust for Historic Preservation made the preservation of national parks a central part of their 2001 National Convention. See also Galen Cranz, *The Politics of Park Design: A History of Urban Parks in America* (Cambridge, MA: The MIT Press, 1989), and Christian Zapatka's *The American Landscape* (New York, NY: Princeton Architectural Press, 1995), which show an interest not only in the aesthetics of the design, but also in the relationship between parks and public policy, economics and social critiques.

**14** The preservation of agricultural structures has been part and parcel of the preservation movement for a long period, but the preservation of the actual land is only now coming under discussion. In Europe, extensive subsidies have maintained much agricultural land, but in such tightly inhabited countries as the Netherlands there is increasing pressure to view agriculture as a way of preserving open space, separate from its economic or resource value. The debate still continues, however, about whether such technological versions of agriculture as greenhouses should be considered landscape. Theo Baart, Tracy Metz and Tjerk Ruimschotel, *Atlas of Change* (Rotterdam: NAi Uitgevers, 2001). In the United States, the debate has concentrated on the depopulation of the central plains, leading the social critics Frank and Deborah Popper to call for the reversion of the area to a buffalo common in 1987. See also Tim Lehman, *Public Value, Private Lands: Farmland, Preservation, Policy, 1933–1985* (Chapel Hill, NC: The University of North Carolina Press, 1995).

**15** To my knowledge, it was Peter Eisenman who first

articulated this notion in *House X* (New York, NY: Rizzoli International Publications, 1982). His move away from architecture as the making of autonomous buildings was set up in his essay "Post-Functionalism" in *Oppositions* (1976). Eisenman later developed his interest in the abstraction of "text" and "texture" directly into structures that might serve as inhabitations in, for example, House Eleven Odd (1983), Romeo and Juliet (Venice Biennale project, 1984), Guardiola House (1988) and several theoretical projects for laboratory and academic buildings during the mid-1980s. He then turned toward an interest in scientific systems at the end of the 1990s. Eisenman also helped spread the views of the French "thinkers" through his leadership at the Institute of Architecture and Urban Studies (IAUS) and through his tireless lecturing. See Jean-François Bedard, ed., *Cities of Artificial Excavation* (New York, NY: Rizzoli International Publications, 1994). The department of comparative literature at Yale University, where Paul de Man and others were teaching, also had a strong influence.

16 Jacques Derrida, *Margins of Philosophy*, trans. Alan Bass (Chicago, IL: The University of Chicago Press, 1984). Two other books by Derrida are *Disseminations*, trans. Barbara Johnson (Chicago, IL: The University of Chicago Press, 1981), and *Writing and Difference*, trans. Alan Bass (Chicago, IL: University of Chicago Press, 1978). For a good synopsis of Derrida's method, see Gregory Ulmer's "The Object of Post-Criticism" in Hal Foster, ed., *The Anti-Aesthetic: Essays on Postmodern Culture* (New York, NY: The New Press, 2002): 83–110. See also Fredric Jameson's *Postmodernism, Or, The Cultural Logic of Late Capitalism* (New York, NY: Verso, 1992). Jameson was the most popular and effective translator of Derrida's ideas to an American academic public. Derrida has collaborated with several architects, but the results have not been noteworthy.

17 See above. The most direct result of Derrida's teaching can be seen in the work of Daniel Libeskind, who by the mid-1980s was producing projects that, like Eisenman's, moved away from the construction of purely abstract, grid-derived forms to the folding and unfolding of what he saw as an invented "ground" or foundation that was almost completely theoretical. See Daniel Libeskind, *Radix-Matrix: Architecture and Writings* (Munich: Prestel Verlag, 1997), and his *Daniel Libeskind: The Space of Encounter* (New York, NY: Universe Publishing, 2001). See, as a retrospective, *Folding in Architecture*, A.D. (vol. 63, 1993), especially the essay by Greg Lynn entitled "Architectural Curvilinearity: The Folded, the Pliant and the Supple": 8–15. The 1988 exhibition at the Museum of Modern Art introduced this way of thinking to the general public. See Mark Wigley's *Deconstructivist Architecture* (New York, NY: The Museum of Modern Art, 1988), and Mark C. Taylor's *Knots* (Chicago, IL: University of Chicago Press, 1993).

18 Mark Wigley. *The Architecture of Deconstruction: Derrida's Haunt* (Cambridge, MA: The MIT Press, 1993).

19 The direct relationship between this suppression and the fact that architecture has such a troubled theoretical foundation was laid by Mark Wigley in "Postmortem Architecture: A Taste of Derrida," *Perspecta* (New York, NY: Rizzoli International Publications, no. 23, 1987): 156–72. See also Mark C. Taylor's *Hiding* (Chicago, IL: University of Chicago Press, 1997), and Anthony Vidler's *The Architectural Uncanny. Essays in the Modern Unhomely*, (Cambridge, MA: The MIT Press, 1992).

20 Martin Heidegger, "Building, Dwelling, Thinking," trans. Albert Hofstadter, *Poetry, Language, Thought* (New York, NY: Harper & Row Publishers, 1971): 143–61.

21 Martin Heidegger, *Early Greek Thinking*, trans. David Farrell Krell and Frank A. Capuzzi (San Francisco, CA: Harper & Row, 1985).

22 Martin Heidegger, *Being and Time*, trans. John Macquarrie and Edward Robinson (London: SCM Press, 1962).

23 Martin Heidegger, *The Question Concerning Technology*, trans. William Lovitt (New York, NY: Harper & Row, 1977): 20.

24 Martin Heidegger, *The Question Concerning Technology*, trans. William Lovitt (New York, NY: Harper & Row, 1977): 18, 32.

25 The group met sporadically, but twelve issues of the magazine *Internationale Situationniste* were published between 1958 and 1969. See Libero Andreotti and Xavier Costa, eds., *Situationists: Art, Politics, Urbanism* (Barcelona: Museé d'Art Contemporaine de Barcelona, 1996), and Guy Debord's *The Society of the Spectacle* (New York, NY: Zone Books, 1994).

26 Libero Andreotti and Xavier Costa, eds., trans. Paul Hammond, *Theory of the Dérive and other Situationist Writings on the City* (Barcelona: Museé d'Art Contemporaine de Barcelona, 1996).

27 Bruce Chatwin, *The Songlines* (London: Jonathan Cape, 1987).

28 Jean-Clarence Lambert, ed., *Constant, New Babylon, Art et Utopie, Textes Situationnistes* (Paris: Cercle d'Art, 1997).

29 Peter Cook et.al., eds., *Archigram* (London: Studio Vista, 1972).

30 There are no full studies yet of the group. See Emilio Ambasz, ed., *Italy: The New Domestic Landscape* (New York, NY: The Museum of Modern Art, 1972).

31 Their work was exhibited by the FRAC Orléans in 2001 in an exhibition entitled "Futurs Antérieurs: Pascal Hauseman, Jean-Louis Chaneac, Antti Lovag," but no catalogue exists.

32 Gilles Deleuze and Felix Guattari, trans. Brian Massumi, *Anti-Oedipus: Capitalism and Schizophrenia* (Minneapolis, MN: University of Minnesota Press, 1989).

33 Gilles Deleuze and Felix Guattari, trans. Brian Massumi, *A Thousand Plateaus: Capitalism and Schizophrenia* (Minneapolis, MN: University of Minnesota Press, 1987).

34 Benoît B. Mandelbort, *The Fractal Geometry of Nature* (New York, NY: W H Freeman & Co., 1982).

35 Ilya Prigogine and Isabelle Stengers, *Order out of Chaos: Man's New Dialogue with Nature* (London: Heinemann, 1984).

36 These theories were heavily propagated during the late 1980s most spectacularly by James Gleick in his *Chaos: Making a New Science* (New York, NY: Viking, 1987). Of particular interest is N. Katherine Hayles's analysis of the different uses to which such theories were put by scientists and academics in *Chaos Bound: Orderly Disorder in Contemporary Literature and Science* (Ithaca, NY: Cornell University Press, 1990). Now that these theories have been absorbed into our culture it is possible to take a critical look at their place in modernist theory in general and to argue for what aspects of non-linearity, fragmentation and non-objective formations might make for an effective architecture. This is done brilliantly by Sanford Kwinter in *Architectures of Time: Toward a Theory of the Event in Modernist Culture* (Cambridge, MA: The MIT Press, 2001).

37 Gilles Deleuze and Felix Guattari, trans. Brian Massumi, *A Thousand Plateaus: Capitalism and Schizophrenia* (Minneapolis, MN: University of Minnesota Press, 1987): 481.

38 Gilles Deleuze and Felix Guattari, trans. Brian Massumi, *A Thousand Plateaus: Capitalism and Schizophrenia* (Minneapolis, MN: University of Minnesota Press, 1987): 444–514.

39 Gilles Deleuze, trans. Tom Conley, *The Fold: Leibniz and the Baroque* (Minneapolis, MN: University of Minnesota Press, 1993).

40 Henri Lefebvre, trans. Donald Nicholson-Smith. *The Production of Space* (Oxford, UK: Blackwell Publishers, 1991).

41 The link between Lefebvre and Sartre, and also between Edmund Husserl and Martin Buber, was laid by Edward Soja in "Reassertions: Towards a Spatialized Ontology," in his book *Postmodern Geographies: The Reassertion of Space in Critical Social Theory* (London: Verso, 1989): 118–37, 132–37.

42 Henri Lefebvre, trans. Donald Nicholson-Smith. *The Production of Space* (Oxford, UK: Blackwell Publishers, 1991): 33–37.

43 Henri Lefebvre, trans. Donald Nicholson-Smith. *The Production of Space* (Oxford, UK: Blackwell Publishers, 1991): 37–40, 125. For a sharpening of the argument, see Edward Soja, *Postmodern Geographies: The Reassertion of Space in Critical Social Theory* (London: Verso, 1989): 121–31.

44 Henri Lefebvre, trans. Donald Nicholson-Smith. *The Production of Space* (Oxford, UK: Blackwell Publishers, 1991): 420–23.

45 J. B. Jackson, "The Moveable Dwelling and How It Came to America," *Landscape in Sight: Looking at America* (New Haven, CT: Yale University Press, 1997): 210–23.

46 Aaron Betsky, *Building Sex: Men, Women, Architecture and the Construction of Sexuality* (New York, NY: William Morrow, 1995).

47 Le Corbusier, trans. Frederick Etchells, *Towards a New Architecture* (London: Architectural Press, 1946): 31.

48 Henri Lefebvre, trans. Donald Nicholson-Smith. *The Production of Space* (Oxford, UK: Blackwell Publishers, 1991): 38–39.

49 Michel Foucault, "Other Spaces: The Principles of Heterotopia," *Lotus* (no. 48/49, 1986): 10–24.

50 Frank Lloyd Wright designed the 12-foot-long model of Broadacre City as a theoretical project originally to be shown in New York at the Rockefeller Center. See Brendan Gill, *Many Masks: A Life of Frank Lloyd Wright* (London: Heinemann, 1988): 334–38.

51 Esther Da Costa Meyer, *The Work of Antonio Sant'Elia: Retreat into the Future* (New Haven, CT: Yale University Press, 1995).

52 Hugh Ferris, *The Metropolis of Tomorrow* (New York, NY: I Washburn, 1929. Reprinted, Princeton, NJ: Princeton Architectural Press, 1998).

53 Alison and Peter Smithson, *Smithson: Team 10 Primer* (Cambridge, MA: The MIT Press, 1975).

54 Donald Albrecht, *Designing Dreams: Modern Architecture in the Movies* (New York, NY: Hennessey & Ingalls, 2000). Dietrich Neumann, ed., *Film Architecture: Set Designs from Metropolis to Blade Runner* (Munich: Prestel Verlag, 1999). Thomas Pynchon, *Vineland* (New York, NY: Minerva, 1991). Thomas Pynchon, *Gravity's Rainbow* (London: Vintage, 1995).

55 Lebbeus Woods, *Radical Reconstruction* (New York, NY: Princeton Architectural Press, 1997). See also Aaron Betsky's essay "Lebbeus Woods," *A+U* (1992).

56 Rosalind Kraus, "Sculpture in the Expanded Field," *October* (no. 8, 1979).

**CHAPTER 1**

1 Alberton Perez-Gomez, *Architecture and the Crisis of Modern Science* (Cambridge, MA: The MIT Press, 1985). Perez-Gomez argues that it was the increasing reliance on abstract science and particularly geometry that divorced architecture from the practicalities of interior design and engineering. One could also argue that such categorization was part of a general trend toward specialization in which architecture was allied with the state in projecting the central images of the executive agencies. Later, it also engaged in planning. In the end, however, as Manfredo Tafuri has pointed out in *Architecture and Utopia: Design and Capitalist Development* (trans. Barbara Luigia La Penta, Cambridge, MA: The MIT Press, 1976), architecture lost its efficacy in both areas. Ironically, architecture was left without a clear task, and this may be the reason why architects are not attempting to integrate interior design and landscape manipulation.

2 For Michael Baxandall, however, all these elements are intricately linked. He is one of the few theoreticians—perhaps because he is outside the architectural profession—to explicitly link engineering, landscape and aesthetic concerns in architecture. See Michael Baxandall, "The Historical Object: Benjamin Baker's Forth Bridge," *Patterns of Intention: On the Historical Explanation of Pictures* (New Haven, CT: Yale University Press, 1985): 12–40.

3 For a discussion of the impact underground culture had on nineteenth-century culture see Wendy Lesser, *The Life Below the Ground: A Study of the Subterranean in Literature and History* (New York, NY: Faber & Faber Inc., 1987).

4 The story is remarkably prophetic considering that it was written in 1908. E.M. Forster, "The Machine Stops," ed. Rod Mengham, *The Machine Stops and Other Stories* (London: André Deutsch, 1997).

5 Willy Boesiger, ed., *Le Corbusier et Pierre Jeanneret: Oeuvre Complete de 1929–1934* (Erlenbach-Zurich: Editions d'Architecture, 1946): 175. See also Mary McLeod, "Le Corbusier in Algiers," *Oppositions* (no. 19/20, 1980): 54–85. Stanislaus von Moos's *Le Corbusier: Elements of a Synthesis* (Cambridge, MA: The MIT Press, 1979): 202–04.

6 Hollein expressed most clearly this fascination with the aircraft carrier in his 1980 coffee set for Alessi. See *Hans Hollein*, an issue of *A+U* (no. 2 supplement, 1985), in which is Kenneth Frampton's essay "Meditations on an Aircraft Carrier": 142–44.

7 This was laid out in the so-called "Athens Charter for the Restoration of Historic Monuments" after CIAM's boat trip to Athens in 1931. See Ulrich Conrads, trans. Michael Bullock, *Programs and Manifestoes on 20th-Century Architecture*, (Cambridge, MA: The MIT Press, 1971): 137–45.

8 Peter and Alison Smithson, *Smithson: Team 10 Primer* (Cambridge, MA: The MIT Press, 1975). Peter and Alison Smithson, *Ordinariness and Light* (New York, NY: Faber & Faber Inc., 1970).

9 For the best discussion of Nieuwenhuis's relationship with the situationists, see Mark Wigley, *Constant's New Babylon: The Hyper-Architecture of Desire* (Rotterdam: 010 Publishers, 1998), and Simon Sadler, *The Situationist City* (Cambridge, MA: The MIT Press, 1998).

10 Jean-Clarence Lambert, ed., *Constant: New Babylon: Art et Utopie* (Paris: Cercle d'Art, 1997).

11 Although American architects turned toward Norbert Wiener's (1894–1964) theory of "cybernetics" at the end of this period, the general belief in the efficacy of overall patterns and structures seemed to come out of a combination of pragmatism (the need to span and plan ever-larger spaces or urban blocks for convention centers and urban redevelopment), a belief in systems, mass production and the notion "bigger is better" that marked the postwar economy.

Many of these theories were published in the first issue (1964), "One," of *World Architecture*. For example, Peter and Alison Smithson called for buildings as "mats" that would combine a number of functions in an open grid with public spaces in-between, and Shadrack Woods looked for a constructional and mathematical system that would arrange complex functions. See also Mary Louise Lobsinger, "Cybernetic Theory and the Architecture of Performance: Cedric Price's fun Palace," Sarah Williams Goldhagen and Rejean Legault, eds., *Anxious Modernisms: Experimentation in Postwar Architectural Culture* (Montreal: Canadian Center for Architecture, 2000): 119–40.

**12** "Architecture + Film I," an issue of *Architectural Design* (1994). Bob Fear, "Therapeutic Visions: James Bond, Stanley Kubrick, Captain Kirk and George Lucas," *Architecture + Film II* (New York, NY: John Wiley & Sons, 2000): 86–95.

**13** Peter Cook et.al., *Archigram* (Basel: Birkhauser Verlag, 1990).

**14** Richard Rogers, *Cities for a Small Planet* (New York, NY: Faber & Faber Inc., 1997). See also Richard Rogers's lecture "The Fragmented City and the Role of the Architect" given on 15 November 2001 at the Fifth Megacities Lecture in The Hague. It is transcribed on the internet at www.megacities.nl/lectures.htm.

**15** Emilio Ambasz, *Architettura Naturale: Progetti e Oggetti* (*Architecture as Nature: Projects and Objects*, Milan: Electa, 1993).

**16** Sorkin's work is the result of years of theorizing and postulating and can be applied to any number of different settings. See Michael Sorkin, *Local Code: The Constitution of a City at 42 Degrees N Latitude* (New York, NY: Princeton Architectural Press, 1993).

**17** Ernest Callenbach, *Ecotopia* (New York, NY: Bantam Books, 1990).

**18** Catherine Slessor and John Linden, *Eco-Tech: Sustainable Architecture and High Technology* (London: Thames & Hudson, 1997).

**19** Good recent surveys of such work include Udo Weilacher, trans. Felicity Gloth, *Between Landscape Architecture and Land Art* (Basel: Birkhauser Verlag, 1999); Sutherland Lyall, *Designing the New Landscape* (London: Thames & Hudson, 1997). See also Aaron Betsky, "Dig We Must: An Argument for Revelatory Landscapes," Aaron Betsky and Leah Levy, eds., *Revelatory Landscapes* (San Francisco, CA: San Francisco Museum of Modern Art, 2001): 8–21.

**20** Lawrence Halprin, *Lawrence Halprin, Process Architecture* (no. 4, 1979). Richard Sexton, *Parallel Utopias. The Sea Ranch, California, Seaside, Florida: The Quest for Community* (San Francisco, CA: Chronicle Books, 1995).

**CHAPTER 2**

**1** For a survey of caves and other underground dwellings see David Kempe, *Living Underground: A History of Cave and Cliff Dwelling* (London: The Herbert Press, 1988). The book surveys the variety and history of underground and semi-underground dwellings around the world, pointing out the environmental and cultural reasons for this building type.

**2** Wendy Lesser, *The Life Below the Ground: A Study of the Subterranean in Literature and Theory* (New York, NY: Faber & Faber Inc., 1987).

**3** Dante's story of coming upon a fissure in the earth, entering to a lower realm and then rising up, reborn and with a new purpose, is of course indebted to a rich history of classical writing. All these types of tales may have some relation to near-death experiences that are supposed to be enlightening, or may be an acting out of dreams. Dante Alighieri, trans. Allen Mandelbaum, *The Divine Comedy* (New York, NY: Everyman's Library, Alfred A. Knopf, 1995). Jules Verne, *Journey to the Centre of the Earth*, trans. William Butcher (New York, NY: Oxford University Press, 1998). In 1938, the architect Giuseppe Terragni (1904–43) designed an architectural equivalent of *The Divine Comedy*, which unfortunately was never built. See Thomas L. Schumacher, *The Danteum: A Study in the Architecture of Literature* (New York, NY: Princeton Architectural Press, 1986).

**4** Aaron Betsky, *Building Sex: Men, Women, Architecture and Construction of Sexuality* (New York, NY: William Morrow, 1995). Mario Praz, *An Illustrated History of Interior Decoration: From Pompeii to Art Nouveau* (London: Thames & Hudson, 1982).

**5** For a survey of Rococo style see Anthony Blunt, *Baroque and Rococo Architecture and Decoration* (London: Elek, 1978). Michael Schwarz, *The Age of the Rococo* (Austin, TX: Holt, Rinehart and Winston, 1971). Katie Scott, *Rococo Interior. Decoration and Social Spaces in Early-Eighteenth-Century Paris* (New Haven, CT: Yale University Press, 1996). William Park, *The Idea of Rococo* (Cranbury, NJ: University of Delaware Press, 1992).

**6** Luigi Ficacci, trans. Bradley Baker Dick, *Piranesi: The Complete Etchings* (Cologne: Benedikt Taschen Verlag, 2000). Manfredo Tafuri, trans. Pellegrino d'Acierno and Robert Connolly, *The Sphere and the Labyrinth: Avant-Gardes and Architecture from Piranesi to the 1970s* (Cambridge, MA: The MIT Press, 1990).

**7** A strange but very complete survey of Lequeu's work, Philippe Duboy, trans. Francis Scarfe, *Lequeu: An Architectural Enigma* (Cambridge, MA: The MIT Press, 1986).

**8** For an interesting perspective on the rediscovery of caves see Mary-Ann Ray, *Seven Partly Underground Rooms and Buildings for Water, Ice, and Midgets* (New York, NY: Princeton Architectural Press, 1997).

**9** For a survey of surrealist art and thought see Jenniver Mundy and Dawn Ades, eds., *Surrealism: Desire Unbound* (London: Tate Gallery Publishing, 2001). For a speculation on the way in which this movement fits into a wider concern for body imagery in architecture see Christian W. Thomsen and Angela Krewani, trans. Alex Atkins, *Sensuous Architecture: The Art of Erotic Building* (Munich: Prestel Verlag, 1998).

**10** Willy Boesiger, *Le Corbusier et Pierre Jeanneret: Oeuvre Complete de 1929–1934* (Erlenbach-Zurich: Editions d'Architecture, 1946): 53–57. Willy Boesiger, *Le Corbusier Oeuvre Complete de 1952–1957* (Zurich: Editions Girsberger, 1957): 206–19.

**11** David B. Brownlee and David G. De Long, *Louis I. Kahn: In the Realm of Architecture* (New York, NY: Rizzoli International Publications, 1991).

**12** Peter Reed, ed., *Alvar Aalto: Between Humanism and*

*Materialism* (New York, NY: The Museum of Modern Art, 1998). In particular, Marc Treib's essay "Aalto's Landscape": 47–67.

**13** Hans Hollein, *Hans Hollein* (Berlin: Ernst & Sohn, 1992).

**14** Peter Arnell and Ted Bickford, eds., *James Stirling Buildings and Projects* (New York, NY: Rizzoli International Publications, 1984): 197–215, 252–60.

**15** For a discussion of the memorial's meaning see Kristin Ann Hass, *Carried to the Wall: American Memory and the Vietnam Veterans Memorial* (Berkeley, CA: University of California Press, 1998).

**16** For an excellent survey see Yegül Fikret, *Baths and Bathing in Classical Antiquity* (New York, NY: Architectural History Foundation, 1992).

**17** Rem Koolhaas, *Delirious New York: A Retroactive Manifesto for Manhattan* (London: Thames & Hudson, 1978).

**18** The most eloquent evocation of this environment comes when Fitzgerald realizes its limitations during the Great Depression. F. Scott Fitzgerald, "My Lost City," *The Crack-Up* (New York, NY: New Directions Publishing, 1968): 23–33.

**19** Lebbeus Woods, *Terra Nova* (Tokyo: A+U Publishing, 1991). Lebbeus Woods, *Anarchitecture: Architecture Is a Political Act* (New York, NY: St Martin's Press, Architectural Monographs, no. 22, 1992).

**CHAPTER 3**

**1** Such strategies are partly inspired by readings in French philosophy. For a survey of folded architecture see "Folding in Architecture" (*Architectural Design*, Profile 102, vol. 63, no. 3/4, 1993).

**2** For a good survey of the Ecole des Beaux-Arts see Arthur Drexler, ed., *The Architecture of the Beaux-Arts* (New York, NY: The Museum of Modern Art, 1977). Robin Middleton, ed., *The Beaux-Arts and Nineteenth-Century French Architecture* (London: Thames & Hudson, 1982). Donald Drew Egbert, ed., *The Beaux-Arts Tradition in French Architecture* (Princeton, NJ: Princeton University Press, 1980).

**3** Frank Lloyd Wright, "Taliesin," Edgar Kaufman, ed., *Frank Lloyd Wright: Writings and Buildings* (New York, NY: Horizon Press, 1960): 171–82.

**4** David G. De Long, *Bruce Goff: Toward Absolute Architecture* (Cambridge, MA: The MIT Press, 1988).

**5** Frank Escher, ed., *John Lautner, Architect* (London: Artemis, 1994).

**6** Predock does not convey his thoughts in writing, but rather in lectures and on his website (www.antoinepredock.com). See *Antoine Predock Architect 1* (New York, NY: Rizzoli International Publications, 1995) and *Antoine Predock Architect Vol. 2* (New York, NY: Rizzoli International Publications, 1998).

**7** Daniel Libeskind, *Daniel Libeskind: The Space of Encounter* (London: Thames & Hudson, 2001).

**8** Aaron Betsky, "Architecture beyond 98 Degrees," *Zaha Hadid: The Complete Buildings and Projects* (London: Thames & Hudson, 1998): 6–15.

**9** Maria Antonietta-Crippa, trans. Susan Chapman and Paola Pinna, *Carlo Scarpa: Theory, Design, Projects*, (Cambridge, MA: The MIT Press, 1986).

**10** James Wines, *De-Architecture* (New York, NY: Rizzoli International Publications, 1987).

**CHAPTER 4**

**1** Noam Chomsky, *Aspects of the Theory of Syntax* (Cambridge, MA: The MIT Press, 1965).

**2** See the discussion about Peter Eisenman in the introduction. Philip Johnson, Robert B. Somol, Charles Jencks and Kurt Forster, *The Wexner Center for the Arts* (New York, NY: St. Martin's Press, 1990).

**3** Greg Lynn, *Animate Form* (New York, NY: Princeton Architectural Press, 1998). See also Greg Lynn, *Folds, Bodies and Blobs: Collected Essays* (Brussels: La Lettre Volée, 1998).

**4** Ben van Berkel and Caroline Bos, *Move* (Goose Press, 1999).

**5** William J. Mitchell, *City of Bits: Space, Place, and the Infobahn* (Cambridge, MA: The MIT Press, 1996). William J. Mitchell, *e-topia: "Urban Life, Jim—But not as We Know It"* (Cambridge, MA: The MIT Press, 2000). Michael L. Benedikt, ed., *Cyberspace: First Steps* (Cambridge, MA: The MIT Press, 1991). John Beckmann, ed., *The Virtual Dimension: Architecture, Representation, and Crash Culture* (New York, NY: Princeton Architectural Press, 1998).

**6** For the best discussion of the garden as artifice see Allen S. Weiss, *Unnatural Horizons: Paradox & Contradiction in Landscape Architecture* (New York, NY: Princeton Architectural Press, 1998). May Woods, *Visions of Arcadia: European Gardens from Renaissance to Rococo* (London: Aurum, 1996).

**7** John Dixon Hunt and Peter Willis, *The Genius of Place: The English Garden Landscape, 1620–1820* (London: Elek, 1975).

**8** For the cultural context of such an attitude see David E. Nye, *American Technological Sublime* (Cambridge, MA: The MIT Press, 1994). For a more in-depth view of the synthesis between planning, large-scale engineering projects and landscape architecture see Phoebe Cutler, *The Public Landscape of the New Deal* (New Haven, CT: Yale University Press, 1985). For an understanding of the marriage of social, infrastructural and aesthetic concerns see Marc Treib, Dorothée Imbert and Garrett Eckbo, *Modern Landscapes for Living* (Berkeley, CA: University of California Press, 1997).

**9** Dan Kiley and Jane Amidon, *Dan Kiley: In His Own Words* (London: Thames & Hudson, 1999).

**10** Rosalind Kraus, "Sculpture in the Expanded Field," *October* (no. 8, 1979).

**11** For a discussion of this relationship see Peter Buchanan, "Return to Mother Earth," *Daidalos* (March, 1993): 50–61. See also Erika Suderberg, ed., *Space, Site, Intervention: Situating Installation Art* (Minneapolis, MN: University of Minnesota Press, 2000). Julie H. Reiss, *From Margin to Center: The Spaces of Installation Art* (Cambridge, MA: The MIT Press, 2000).

**12** Gary Shapiro, *Earthworks: Robert Smithson and Art After Babel* (Berkeley, CA: University of California Press, 1997). Robert Carleton Hobbs, *Robert Smithson: Sculpture* (Ithaca, NY: Cornell University Press, 1982).

**13** Germano Celant, *Michael Heizer* (Milan: Fondazione Prada, 1991).

**14** Julia Brown, ed., *Occluded Front: James Turrell* (Fellows of Contemporary Art, Los Angeles and the Lapis Press, 1985).

**15** Walter de Maria, *Walter de Maria: The 5•7•9 Series* (New York: Gagosian Gallery, 1992).

**16** Peter Noever, ed., *Donald Judd: Architecture* (Ostfildern, Germany: Hatje Cantz Verlag, 2002).

**17** Brooke Hodge, ed., *Not Architecture but Evidence that Architecture Exists: Lauretta Vinciarelli: Watercolors* (New York, NY: Princeton Architectural Press, 1999).

**18** Steven Holl, "Within the City: Phenomena of Relations, The Porta Vittoria Project," *Design Quarterly* (no. 39, 1988): 5–32.

**19** Steven Holl, *Edge of a City* (New York, NY: Princeton Architectural Press, 1998).

# ILLUSTRATION CREDITS

**20** Rem Koolhaas, *Delirious New York: A Retroactive Manifesto for Manhattan* (London: Thames & Hudson, 1979).

**21** The group is only loosely organized, but publishes, teaches and sometimes works together. Its main theorist is Manuel Gausa. Especially useful is his essay "Arquitectura Es (Ara) Geografia/Altras 'Natures' Urbanes," *Otras "Naturalezas" Urbanas: Arquitectura Es (Ahora) Geografia (Other Urban Natures: Architecture is (now) Geography*, Espai d'Art Contemporani de Castello, 2001): 16–37.

Art © Donald Judd Foundation/VAGA, New York/DACS, London 2002 141 [left]
Behnisch, Behnisch & Partner, photographer:
Martin Schodder 120–21
Hélène Binet 88, 89 [top]
William Bruder 86–87
© ADAGP, Paris and DACS, London 2002 25 [middle row, second from left] 38–39
© ARS, NY and DACS, London 2002 98 [right]
© DACS 2002 10 [right], 19 [right], 105 [middle row, far right], 124–25
© FLC/ADAGP, Paris and DACS, London 2002 18 [right], 59 [left]
Courtesy of the artist, Maya Lin 72 [top], 73
Courtesy of the National Park Service 72 [bottom]
Dan Wells © The Cosanti Foundation 12 [middle], 20 [left]
Richard Davies 3, 4, 26–27
M. Deuancé 55 [top right]
Yves Eigenmann, Fribourg 95 [bottom]
Peter Eisenman 9, 138
Sverre Fehn 61
François et Associés 174–75
Fregoso + Basalto 55 [left, bottom right]
Mitsumasa Fujitsuka 130, 131 [left and bottom right]
Massimiliano Fuksas 90, 91 [bottom right]
Aki Furudate 91 [bottom left]
Lawrence Halprin 23 [left]
Michael Heizer 140 [right]
Hiroshi Ueda/*Japan Architect* 68–69, 74
Timothy Hursley 13 [right], 103, 112–13, 116–17, 128–29, 146–49, 158–59
David Joseph 156–57
Aaron Kiley 140 [left]
Toshiharu Kitajima 56, 66–67
Kozlowski 90–91
Annette LeCuyer 77 [left column]

Map System Company 16, 50
Michael Sorkin Studio 22 [right], 40–41
Mitsuo Matsuoka Photographer Office 75 [top]
Michael Moran 102 [right], 118–19
Jeroen Musch 46–47
Musei Civici, Como 12 [left]
Florian Musso, Sion 94
Nigel Young/Foster and Partners 32–33
Njiric & Njiric 164–65
Norihiko Dan Office 131 [top right]
Kuoji Okamoto 49 [right]
Photos courtesy of Hargreave Associates 30–31
Heinz Preisig, Sion 95 [top]
Renzo Piano Building Workshop 54
Christian Richters 8, 38–39, 42–45, 60 [right], 70–71, 78–81, 100 [right], 106–07, 108–09, 122–23, 143 [left, right], 144, 150–51, 168–71, 176
Sally Schoolmaster 141 [right], 162–63
Filippo Simonetti 96, 132–33
SITE Projects, Inc. 104
Steven Holl Architects 142 [right], 172–73
Studio Shun 51
Superstudio 10 [left]
Hisao Suzuki 76, 77 [right], 84–85, 101, 126–27
Tomio Ohashi Photographer Office 75 [middle and bottom]
Jocelyne Van den Bossche 36–37, 136, 154–55
Hiromi Watanabe 49 [left]
Kim Zwarts 89 [bottom]

# PROJECT CREDITS

## CHAPTER 1

### HOUSE IN WALES
UK, 1998
Architect **Future Systems**
Structural engineer **Teckniker**
Services engineer **BDSP**

### CORRUGATED DUCT HOUSE
Palm Springs, California, US, 1998
Architect **Neil M. Denari Architects**
Project team **Neil Denari, Jae Shin**
Area **2,700 sq ft (251m²)**

### GUADALUPE RIVER PARK
San José, California, US, 1994–present
Architect **Hargreaves Associates**
Design director **George Hargreaves**
Project team **Glenn Allen, Tim Baird, Chris Fannin, Peter Geraghty, Hiroki Hasegawa, Jeff Hodgson, Mary Margaret Jones, David Jung, Andrzej Karwacki, Kurt Lango, Eric Pfeiffer, Pariya Sheanakul, Dah-Win Sheu, Ramsey Silberberg, Dennis Taniguchi, Gail Wittwer**
Client. **San Jose Redevelopment Agency in association with US Army Corps of Engineers, Santa Clara Valley Water District, and Santa Clara County**
Hydraulic and structural engineer **AN West**
Civil and geotechnical engineer **AGS, Inc.**
Electrical engineer **MTH, Inc.**
Environmental consultant **H.T. Harvey Associates**
Contractor **b&b Concrete** (phase 1)

### GREAT GLASS HOUSE
National Botanic Garden of Wales, Carmarthenshire, Wales, UK, 1995–2000
Architect **Foster and Partners**
Client **National Botanic Garden of Wales**

Landscape architects **Colvin and Moggridge, Gustafson Porter**
Structural engineer **Anthony Hunt Associates**
Mechanical and electrical engineer **Max Fordham & Partners**
Consultants **Schal International, Symonds Ltd**
Area **62,433 sq ft (5,800m²)**

### SPRINGTECTURE A
Aomori Prefecture, Japan, 2000
Architect **Shuhei Endo**
Client **Aomori Prefecture**
Principal use **museum**
Structural system **PCaPC**
Area **99,354 sq ft (9,230m²)**

### TERRASSON GREENHOUSE
Terrasson-la-Villedieu, Dordogne, France, 1992–96
Architect **Ian Ritchie Architects**
Project team **I. Ritchie, S. Conolly, E. Wan**
Client **Municipality of Terrasson**
Landscape architect **Kathryn Gustafson/Paysage Land Paris**
Construction management and concrete and services engineer **Arc Engineering, Brives**
Steelwork engineer **Ove Arup & Partners, London**
Lighting **Ian Ritchie Architects**

### HOUSE OF THE FUTURE
Architect **Michael Sorkin Studio**
Project team **Michael Sorkin and Andrei Vovk**

### WATER PAVILION
Neeltje Jans, the Netherlands, 1997
Architect **NOX/Lars Spuybroek**
Project team **Joan Almekinders, Pieter Heymans, Maurice Nio, William Veerbeek**
Interactive design installations **Lars Spuybroek**
Composer **Victor Wentinck**

Sensor development **Bert Bongers**
Lighting **euroGenie, Laurens van Manen, Mathijs van Manen** (hardware), **Floris van Manen** (software)
Projections **Instituut Calibre, Walther Roelen** (ripples), **Jo Mantelers** (wave), **Daniel Dekkers** (blob)

### SECRET GARDEN
Malmö Festival, Malmö, Sweden, 2001
Architect **West 8**
Project team **Rudolf Eilander, Adriaan Geuze, Guido Marsille, Sabine Müller**
Client **Bo01 City of Tomorrow**

### FUKUOKA PREFECTURAL INTERNATIONAL HALL
Fukuoka, Japan, 1995–99
Architect and principal **Emilio Ambasz**
Project director **Hidetoshi Kawaguchi**
Design team **Humberto Cordero, Karen McEvoy, Rizal Oei, Hideo Tanai**
Client **Dai-ichi Mutual Life Insurance Co., Mitsui Real Estate and Fukuoka Prefecture**
Conceptual design phase **Emilio Ambasz, Takenaka Corporation and Nihon Sekkei**
Detail design and supervision phase **Takenaka Corporation & Nihon Sekkei**
Model maker **Peter Ydeen**
Illustrator **Suns Hung**

### MIYAGI STADIUM
Rifu-cho, Miyagi, Sendai Prefecture, 1993–2000
Architect **Hitoshi Abe and Syouichi Haryu Architect Joint Design Office**
Structural engineers **SDG (design period), Kozo Keikaku Engineering (construction period)**
Mechanical engineer **Sogo Consultant**
Landscape engineer **Sano Consultant**
General contractor **Kajima/Okumura/Hashimoto/Okuda JV**
Area **620,022 sq ft (57,600m²)**

### RAYBOULD HOUSE
Fairfield County, Connecticut, US, 1997
Architect **Kolatan/Mac Donald Studio**
Principals **Sulan Kolatan, William Mac Donald**
Project team **Jonathan Baker, Sung Kim, Seungki Min, Jose Sanchez, Erich Schoenenberger**
Client **Robin Raybould**
Engineers **Büro Happold Engineers, Andre Chaszar and Angus Palmer New York**
Contractors **Tri-State Urethane, Gene Palffy**
Area **1,600 sq ft (149m²)**

### PUNTA NAVE BUILDING
Genoa, Italy, 1989–91
Architect and client **Renzo Piano Building Workshop**
Design associates **S. Ishida, F. Marano**
Project team **M. Cattaneo, M. Lusetti, M. Nouvion**
Collaborators **M. Carroll, R. V. Truffelli, M. Varratta**
Soil engineers **A. Bellini, L. Gattoronchieri**
Structural consultant **P. Costa**
Landscaping consultant **M. Desvigne**
Bionic research consultant **C. Di Bartolo**

## CHAPTER 2

### KAZE-NO-OKA CREMATORIUM
Nakatsu, Japan, 1997
Architect **Fumihiko Maki**
Project team **Hiromi Kouda, Yukitoshi Wakatsuki,
Norio Yokota**
Client **Nakatsu City Government**
Contractors **Tobishima Corporation, Toda
Corporation**
Structural engineer **Hanawa Structural Engineering**
Mechanical engineer **Sogo Consultant**
Landscape consultant **Sasaki Environment
Design Office**
Area **24,317 sq ft (2,259m²)**

### HOMPUKUJI WATER TEMPLE
Awaji Island, Japan, 1989–91
Architect **Tadao Ando**
Area **9,257 sq ft (860m²)**

### MINNAERT BUILDING
University of Utrecht, the Netherlands, 1994–98
Architect **Neutelings Riedijk**
Principals **Willem Jan Neutelings, Michiel Riedijk**
Project team **Jago van Bergen, Evert Crols, Burton
Hamfelt, Joost Mulders, Chidi Onwuka, Gerrit Schilder,
Jonathan Woodroffe**

### VIETNAM VETERANS MEMORIAL
Washington, D.C., US, 1980–82
Architect **Maya Lin**
Sponsor **Vietnam Veterans Memorial Fund**
Architect of record **Cooper-Lecky Partnership**
Landscape architect **Henry Arnold**
General contractor **Gilbane Construction**

### NAOSHIMA CONTEMPORARY ART MUSEUM
Kagawa Prefecture, Japan, 1988–95

Architect **Tadao Ando**
Area **26,566 sq ft (2,468m²)**

### IGUALADA CEMETERY
Barcelona, Spain, 1985–96
Architect **Enric Miralles and Carme Pinós**
Building direction **Enric Miralles**
Project team **Joan Callis, Se Duch, Albert Ferré,
Josep Miàs, Eva Prats**

### THERMAL BATHS
Vals, Switzerland, 1990–96
Architect **Peter Zumthor**
Project team **Thomas Durisch, Marc Löliger,
Rainer Weischies**
Building supervision **Franz Bärtsch**
Client **Town of Vals**
Structural engineer **Jürg Buchli, Casanova +
Blumenthal**
Services **Meierhans + Partner**
Area **18,838 sq ft (1750m²)**

### LARRENGUADE TUNNEL
Larrenguade, France, 1994
Architect **François et Associés**
Graphic design **Duncan Lewis**

### MULTIMEDIA WORKSHOP
Ooqaki, Gifu Prefecture, Japan, 1996–97
Architect **Kazuyo Sejima + Ryue Nishizawa/SANAA**
Principals-in-charge **Ryue Nishizawa, Kazuyo Sejima**
Project team **Yoshitaka Tanase, Toshihiro Yoshimura**
Structural engineer **Sasaki Structural Consultants**
Mechanical engineers **System Design Laboratory,
ES Associates, Otaki E&M Consultant**
Area **9,214 sq ft (856m²)**

### VILLA WILBRINK
Amersfoort, the Netherlands, 1992–94

Architect **UN Studio**
Client **Mr and Mrs Wilbrink van den Berg**
Project team **Ben van Berkel** (architect), **Aad
Krom** (project management), **Paul van der Erve,
Branimir Medic**
Building contractor **Aannemersmaatschappij
ABM, Amersfoort**
Constructor **Bureau Bouwpartners, Hilversum**

### NELSON-ATKINS MUSEUM OF ART EXPANSION
Kansas City, Missouri, US, 2000–present
Architect **Steven Holl**
Partner-in-charge **Chris McVoy**
Project architects **Martin Cox, Richard Tobias**
Project team **Gabriela Barman-Kramer, Matthias Blass,
Robert Edmonds, Makram El-Kadi, Mimi Hoang, Li Hu,
Fabian Llonch, Stephen O'Dell, Susi Sanchez, Olaf
Schmidt, Urs Vogt, Christian Wassmann**
Client **Nelson-Atkins Museum of Art**
Associate architect **BNIM**
Area **160,000 sq ft (14,864m²), plus 500-car garage**

### HYDROELECTRIC PLANT
Bieudron, Switzerland, 1995–99
Architect **Claudine Lorenz, Florian Musso**
Client **GD & EOS (Grande-Dixence SA et Energie
Ouest Suisse)**
Coordinators **Cleuson-Dixence, Sion**
Structural engineer **CVI-BG (Communauté Valaisanne
d'Ingénieurs et Bonnard & Gardel)**

## CHAPTER 3

### TRAM TERMINAL
Strasbourg, France, 1999–2001
Architect **Zaha Hadid**
Project architect **Stéphane Hof**
Sketch design team **Stéphane Hof, Sara Klomps,
Sonia Villaseca, Woody K.T. Yao**
Project team **Eddie Can, Markus Dochantschi, Chris
Dopheide, Silvia Forlati, David Gerber, Stanley Lau,
David Salazar, Patrik Schumacher, Caroline Voet**
Client **C.T.S.(Compagnie des Transports
Strasbourgeois)**
Project consultants **Mayer Bährle, Roland Mayer**
Structural engineer **Dr. Ing. Luigi Martino**
Contact architect **Albert Grandadam**
Area **32,293 sq ft (3000m²)**

### CENTRAL LIBRARY
Technical University of Delft, the Netherlands,
1992–98
Architect **Mecanoo**
Project team **Monica Adams, Marjolijn Adriaansche,
Jan Bekkering, Carlo Bevers, Henk Bouwer, Gerrit
Bras, Birgit de Bruin, Ard Buijsen, Katja van Dalen,
Annemiek Diekman, Ineke Dubbledam, Erick van
Egeraat, Aart Fransen, Francine Houben, Alfa
Hügelmann, Axel Koschany, Theo Kupers, Maartje
Lammers, Paul Martin Lied, Bas Streppel, Astrid
van Vliet, Chris de Weijer**
Client **ing Vastgoed Ontwikkeling b.v., Den Haag,
Technische Universiteit, Delft**
Structural engineer **ABT**
Mechanical engineer **Ketel**
Electrical engineer **Deerns**
Area **161,464 sq ft (15,000m²)**

**CASA VERDE**
Pozuelo, Spain, 1997
Architect **Abalos + Herreros**
Project team **Iñaki Abalos, Juan Herreros,**
**Angel Jaramillo**
Collaborators **Auxiliadora Gálvez, Carmen Izquierdo,**
**Carolina González Vives**
Structural engineer **Juan Gómez**
Computer graphics **Gestalt**
Quantity surveyor **Miguel Angel Rica**

**DIAMOND RANCH HIGH SCHOOL**
Pomona, California, us, 1994–99
Architect **Morphosis**
Principal **Thom Mayne**
Project architect **John Enright**
Project team **Cameron Crockett, David Grant, Fabian**
**Kremkus, Janice Shimizu, Patrick J. Tighe**
Project assistants **Sarah Allan, Kaspar Baumeister, Jay**
**Behr, John Bencher, Mark Briggs, Frank Brodbeck,**
**Takashi Ehira, Magdalena Glen, Ivar Gudmunson,**
**George Hernandez, Martin Krammer, Ming Lee,**
**Francisco Mouzo, Christopher Payne, Kinga Racon,**
**Robyn Sambo, Andreas Schaller, Bennet Shen, Mark**
**Sich, Craig Shimahara, Tadao Shimizu, Steve Slaughter,**
**Brandon Welling, Eui-Sung Yi**
Client **Pomona Unified School District**
Associate architect **Thomas Blurock Architects**
Landscape architect **Allen Don Fong**
Structural engineer **Ove Arup & Partners**
Civil engineer **Andreasen Engineering**
General contractor **Bernards Brothers**

**MUSEUM OF THE EARTH**
Ithaca, New York, us, 1999–present
Architect **Weiss/Manfredi Architects**
Principals **Marion Weiss and Michael Manfredi**
Project manager **Christopher Ballentine**
Project team **Lauren Crahan, Armando Petruccelli**

Client **Paleontological Research Institution**
Structural consultants **Weidlinger Associates, Inc.**
MEPFP **MG Engineering p.c. in affiliation with MGJ**
**Associates, Inc.**
Civil engineer **TG Miller, p.c.**
Landscape design **Elemental Landscapes**
Exhibition consultant **Jeff Kennedy Associates, Inc.**
Lighting **Brandston Partnership Inc.**

**SPENCER THEATER**
Ruidoso, New Mexico, us, 1994-97
Architect **Antoine Predock Architect**
Principal-in-charge **Antoine Predock**
Senior-associates-in-charge **Geoffrey Beebe,**
**Douglas Friend**
Project team **Jorge Burbano, Michele Cohen,**
**Devendra Contractor, Mark Donahue, W. Anthony**
**Evanko, Paul Gonzales, Thea Hahn, Georgina Kish,**
**Jennifer Lein, Robert McElheney, Lawrence Mead,**
**John Morrow, George Newlands, Hadrian Predock,**
**Kira Sowanick, Deborah Waldrip**
Client **Spencer Theater for the Performing Arts**
**Foundations**
Contractor **PCL Construction Services, Inc.**
Structural engineer **Robin E. Parke Associates, Inc.**
Mechanical engineer **P2RS Group, Inc.**
Electrical engineer **Telcon Engineering, Inc.**
Civil engineer **Red Mountain Engineers**
Acoustic consultant **McKay Conant Brook, Inc.**
Theater consultant **Fisher/Dachs Associates**
Area **52,000 sq ft (4,831m²)**

**NEUROSCIENCES INSTITUTE**
La Jolla, California, us, 1992–96
Architect **Tod Williams and Billie Tsien**
**Architects**
Principals **Tod Williams and Billie Tsien with**
**Joseph Wong Design Associates**
Project architect **David van Handel**

Project team **Peter Arnold, Matthew Baird, Peter**
**Burns, Betty Chen, Brett Ettinger, Martin Finio,**
**Erika Hinrichs, Matthew Pickner, Vivian Wang**
Structural engineer **Severud Associates**
Mechanical engineer **Tsuchiyama, Kaino & Gibson**
Electrical engineer **Randall Lamb Associates**

**INSTITUTE FOR FORESTRY AND NATURE RESEARCH**
Wageningen, the Netherlands, 1998
Architect **Behnisch, Behnisch & Partner**
Partner-in-charge **Stefan Behnisch**
Project leader **Ton Gilissen**
Project team **Andreas Ditschuneit, Yianni Doulis,**
**Brook Muller, Ken Radtkey, Martin Schodder,**
**Martin Werminghaussen**
Structural engineer **Arohnson Consulting Engineers**
Mechanical engineer **Deerns Consulting Engineers**
Energy engineer **Fraunhofer Institute for Building**
**Physics**
Acoustic engineer **DGMR Consulting Engineers**
Interior garden planning **Copijn Tuin en Landschaps**
**Architecten**
Contractor **Dura-Bouw**
Wood façades **DeGroot Vroomshoop**
High-efficiency glazing **Al van Veen Glasspecialist**
Single-glazed skylights **Pilkington**
Greenhouse roofing **Prins Bleyswijk**

**LANDESGARTENSCHAU PAVILION**
Weil am Rhein, Germany, 1996–99
Architect **Zaha Hadid with Patrik Schumacher and**
**Mayer Bährle**
Project architect **Markus Dochantschi**
Project team **Oliver Domeisen, Wassim Halabi, James**
**Lim, Garin O'Avazian, Barbara Pfenningsdorf**
Client **Landesgartenschau Weil am Rhein 1999**
**GmbH, City of Weil am Rhein, Germany**
Models **Jim Heverin, Jon Richards, June Tamura,**
**Ademir Volic**

Structural consultant **Dr. Ing L. Martino, Grenzach-**
**Wyhlen/Turin**
Area **9,096 sq ft (845 m²)**

**ARCHERY RANGE**
Barcelona, Spain, 1989–92
Architect **Enric Miralles and Carme Pinós**
Project team **Albert Ferré, Eva Prats, Rodrigo Prats**
Building direction **Enric Miralles, Silvia Martinez**

**AMERICAN HERITAGE CENTER AND ART MUSEUM**
University of Wyoming, Laramie, Wyoming, us, 1986–93
Architect **Antoine Predock Architect**
Principal-in-charge **Antoine Predock**
Associate-in-charge **Geoffrey Beebe**
Project architect **Derek Payne**
Project team **Jon Anderson, Jorge Burbano, Phyllis**
**Cece, Linda Christensen, Eileen Devereux, John**
**Flemming, Paul Gonzales, Lorraine Guthrie, David**
**Hrabel, Ron Jacob, Peter Karsten, Pedro Marquez, Brett**
**Oaks, Hadrian Predock, Chris Purvis, Rebecca Riden,**
**Chris Romero, Rob Romero, David Somoza, Sam**
**Sterling, Jeff Wren**
Client **University of Wyoming**
Consulting architect **Pouppirt Architects, Cheyenne,**
**Wyoming—Rande Pouppirt** (principal-in-charge),
**Rebecca Wiegman** (project representative)
University architect **Roger Baalman**
Landscape architect **Antoine Predock**
Construction manager **Mark Shively**
Contractor **Kloefkoen-Ballard Construction**
Structural engineer **Robin E. Parke Associates, Inc.**
Mechanical engineer **Bridgers & Paxton**
Electrical engineer **Tierra del Sol Engineering**
Civil engineer **Chavez-Grieves Consulting**
**Engineers, Inc.**
Estimating consultant **Jerry Pope**
Security consultant **E.B. Brown**
Area **130,000 sq ft (12,077m²)**

**HIYOSHI COMMUNITY CENTER**
Hiyoshi, Kyoto Prefecture, Japan, 1995–98
Architect **Norihiko Dan and Associates**
Client **Town of Hiyoshi**
Structural engineer **Yutaka Aoki**
Mechanical engineer **Ulti Inoue**
Area **70,944 sq ft (6590m²)**

**ELECTRICAL SUBSTATION**
Albanatscha, Switzerland, 1993–96
Architect **Hans-Joerg Ruch**
Client **Raetia Energy, Poschiavo**
Collaborator **Roland Malgiaritta**
Structural engineers **Edy Toscano AG, Pontresina** (inner shell); **Branger + Conzett AG, Churfor** (stone wall)

**ADIDAS CAMPUS**
Herzogenaurach, Germany, 2000–present
Architect and urban planning **Angélil/Graham**
Project team **Marc Angélil, Sarah Graham, Manuel Scholl** (partners-in-charge); **Mark Burkhard, Thomas Hildebrand, Anna Klingmann, Rüdiger Kreiselmayer, Marcel Mathis, Christian Meili, Philipp Röösli**
Clients **Adidas-Salomon AG, Herzogenaurach; Stadt Herzogenaurach; GEV Grundstücksgesellschaft mbH & Co. KG, Herzogenaurach**
Building forms **Marco Ganz, Künstler © 1999 by ProLitteris, Zürich**
Landscape architects **Vetsch Nipkow Partner Landschaftsarchitekten, Zürich; Gnüchtel-Triebswetter Landschaftsarchitekten, Kassel**
Infrastructural planning **H.P. Gauff Ingenieure GmbH & Co, Nürnberg**
Noise control **W. Sorge, Ingenieurbüro for Bauphysik GmbH, Nürnberg**
Building consultants and competition organizers **Hans-Peter Achatzi and Benjamin Hosbach [phase one], Berlin**

**CHAPTER 4**

**RODEN CRATER**
Flagstaff, Arizona, US, 1972–present
Artist **James Turrell**
Architect **Paul D. Bustamonte**
Consulting architects **Skidmore, Owings and Merrill**
Management **Skystone Foundation**
Project management **Tom McGrath**
Astronomer **Dick Walker**
Planning **A...XYZ**

**DUTCH PAVILION**
Hanover Expo, Germany, 1999–2000
Architect **MVRDV**
Project team **Winy Maas, Nathalie de Vries and Jacob van Rijs with Kristina Adsersen, Rüdiger Kreiselmayer, Christoph Schindler, Jaap van Dijk, Stefan Witteman**
Concept phase **Winy Maas, Nathalie de Vries and Jacob van Rijs with Joost Grootens, Christelle Gualdi, Philipp Oswalt, Eline Strijkers, Martin Young**

**NICE TRAMWAY TERMINAL**
Nice, France, 1999–2001
Architect **Marc Barani**
Client **City of Nice, Mission Tramway**
Concept team **KINICIS, Semaly, Public Transportation Engineering; AABD, Bruno Dumetier; Atelier des Paysages, Alain Marguerit**
Project architect **Cyril Chênebeau**
Project team **Julie Assus, Bertrand Charpentier, Pierrandré Conte, Stéphane Fernandez, Erik Jensen, Antoine Lacronique, Michel Pautrel, Emanuelle Pissety, Marianne Rougé, Ivry Serres, VéroniqueToussaint, Monique Vié**
Engineer **SUDEQUIP**
Area **678,149 sq ft (63,000m²)**

**CRYSTAL PALACE CONCERT PLATFORM**
Bromley, London, 1996–97
Architect **Ian Ritchie Architects**
Project team **I. Ritchie, S. Conolly, H. Von Meier**
Client **London Borough of Bromley**
General contractor **Ballast Wiltshier**
Specialist steel contractor **Van Dam**
Structural engineer **Atelier 1, London**
Services engineer **Atelier 10, London**
Acoustics **Paul Gillieron Acoustic Design**
Lighting **Ian Ritchie Architects with Atelier 10**
Landscape architect **Ian Ritchie Architects with London Borough of Bromley**
Quantity surveyors **Quantity Surveying Partnership, London**

**DUNESCAPE**
P.S.1, New York, 2000
Architect **SHoP**
Partners **Kimberly Holden, Gregg Pasquarelli, Coren Sharples, Christopher Sharples, William Sharples**
Project team **Richard Garber, Jonathan Mallie, Kensuke Watanabe**
Fabrication team **Jonathan Mallie** (site project manager), **Jonathan Baker, Roberto Biaggi, Aaron Campbell, Keith Kaseman, Kristopher Lawson, Jamie Palazzolo, Michael Russo**
Structural engineer **Büro Happold**
Contractor **SHoP/Sharples Holden Pasquarelli**

**DOMINUS WINERY**
Yountville, California, US, 1996–98
Architect **Herzog & de Meuron**
Partners-in-charge **Pierre de Meuron, Jacques Herzog**
Project architect **Jean-Frédéric Luscher**
Project team **Uli Ackva, Ines Huber, Nathalie Kury, Mario Meier**
Associate architect **Valley Architects**

Structural engineer **Zucco Fagent Associates**
Mechanical engineer **Larkin Associates**
Electrical engineer **Hansen & Slaughter**
General contractor **Wright Contracting**

**CITY OF CULTURE**
Santiago de Compostela, Spain, 1999–present
Architect **Peter Eisenman**
Client **Department of Culture, Social Communication and Tourism**
Area **2,282,024 sq ft (212,000m²)**

**MARYHILL NATURE OVERLOOK**
Goldendale, Washington, US, 1997–99
Architect **Allied Works Architecture**
Client **Maryhill Museum of Art**
Principal/designer **Brad Cloepfil**
Project manager **Corey Martin**
Structural engineer **Ang Engineering Group**
General contractor **Hard Rock Concrete**
Area **1,206 sq ft (112m²)**

**DENIA CASTLE CULTURAL PARK**
Denia, Spain, 2001
Architect **Vicente Guallart**
Collaborators, phase one **Pilar Gasque, Cristine Bleicher, Barbara Oelbrandt, Marko Brajovic, Laura Cantarella, Giovanni Franceschelli, Maurizio Bonizzi, Silvia Bianchini**
Collaborators, phase two **Jordi Mansilla, Max SanJulian, Li-An Tsien**
Client **The City of Denia (Alicante)**
Collage **Eric Seguin**
Model **Adrià Maynes**
Legal consultant **Alber Cortina (DTUM)**
Area **645,856 sq ft (60,000 m²)**

**BIBLIOTHECA ALEXANDRINA**
Alexandria, Egypt, 1990–2001

# INDEX

These landscrapers give us back the land and architecture. By making us aware of the ground we inhabit, we can regain a sense of the reality of place in a culture that is more and more dependent on the abstraction engendered by the mass production of real and virtual spaces, instant communication, and digital manipulation.